Mark in Time

Disclaimer: This book talks about events and people as I remember them. This does not make it factually accurate and I recognise that others may have different recollections. I may also have embellished events for the sake of a more entertaining read. I make no apology for this.

This book is not a full autobiography and those looking for insight into my motivations and life choices will not necessarily find them here. So, let me say here, just once, I acknowledge that in the twists and turns of my life I have hurt those dearest to me and I do apologise for that.

The book is dedicated to Mum who sadly passed away on the 12th January 2023 but who got to enjoy reading the history in here.

Contents

A life

Timeline

Growing Up

Work

Technology

The Now Years

People and Places

Introduction

My name is Mark Hampson, né Simon Mark Hampson, born 10.5.63 and yes, I am a secret Simon! These are some of the moments that make up my life.

I have been a son, a little brother, a big brother, a friend, a lover, a husband and a father. I have been lucky to be loved throughout my life and to have enjoyed excellent health, surely the most important gifts anyone can receive.

I have also had a career which made me and my family comfortable but also took me to some amazing places, to meet and work with some surprisingly high-profile people and to do some pretty cool things with technology. I enjoy solving problems with technology but mostly through working with others. There has also been time for humour in my line of work (this is important to me) and with a handful of exceptions the people I've worked with have been great, indeed many of my colleagues have also become friends.

So why am I writing this now, and who is it for? Well, I am 58 which is, of course, not old by today's standards. Nonetheless, and in common with most people I know of my age, things do not "mend" as quickly as they used to. And frankly you just can't tell what's around the corner (I started this book immediately before the COVID-19 pandemic broke out!) Of particular relevance to this exercise, memory is most certainly not an infallible tool and I would like to get down in writing at least some of the brilliant moments of my life before they slip from view. To answer the other half of my question, I guess this is primarily for myself, a self-indulgence if you will. I've always enjoyed re-reading things I've written, which certainly doesn't mean I assume others do too! That said, I trust it will be of at least some interest to my daughters and the other special people in my life.

And whether this is vanity, or simply a misguided sense of self- importance, I think at least some of the moments might be of interest to others who do not know me so well. Perhaps time will tell.

Which really leaves just the one important and currently unresolved question which I am sure I should answer before writing this; "what sort of book is this?" At the outset I think this is primarily a summary of important and exciting moments in my working life (people I met, places I've been) with a nod to my personal life rather than a full autobiography, or maybe it will be something in between.

Perhaps now might be a good time to provide some sense of what's to come and why I felt the urge to do this. As a simple northern lad who grew up in East Lancashire and attended a (frankly excellent) grammar school in Yorkshire I didn't really expect to have:

- Received a degree from Oxford University
- Worked at the European Space Agency
- Lived and worked in Germany and Malaysia
- Worked at Logica (at the time one of the finest and most innovative companies in the world), SciSys (a smaller version of Logica!) and the Satellite Applications Catapult
- Been a Programmer, a Team Leader, a Project Manager, an Operations Director, a Chief Executive Officer, a Chief Innovation Officer and an unofficial diplomat/ambassador
- Worked on projects for Space, Defence and Government with customers and partners around the world
- Worked on projects with the United Nations, Red Cross, World Wildlife Fund, Foreign and Commonwealth Office and UK Space Agency
- Played cricket at Trent Bridge, tennis at Wimbledon, golf at posh golf courses and watched rugby at Twickenham

And perhaps most surprisingly, I have met with:

- Princes
- Ministers (at home and abroad)
- A Vice President (and in touching distance of a president)
- A deputy Prime Minister
- Ambassadors
- Astronauts
- City Investors and Philanthropists
- Senior civil servants and scientists
- Hollywood superstars
- Rockstars
- Gerry Anderson
- And one God Emperor....

Timeline

Like most people, my life can be defined, sliced and diced in a number of ways. I have chosen the following breakdown as my work-life is the focus of this book and my personal life has largely aligned with my career steps as shown below. Of course, love and family are more important than work, but we are also defined by our work, or at least I feel I am!

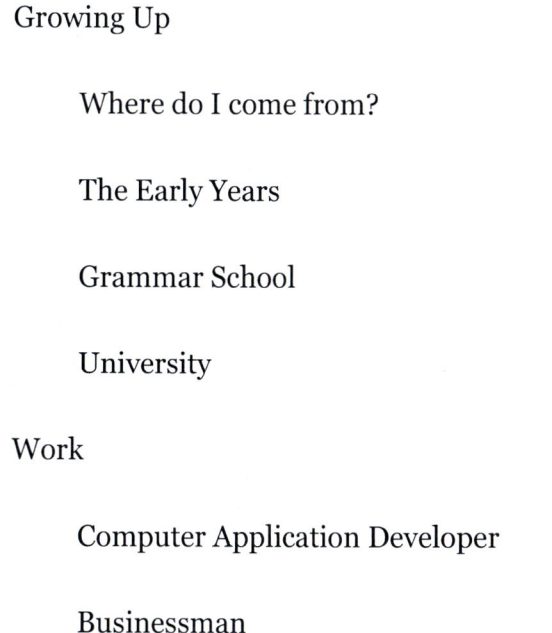

Growing Up

    Where do I come from?

    The Early Years

    Grammar School

    University

Work

    Computer Application Developer

    Businessman

    Innovator & Ambassador

The Now Years

Growing Up

Where Do I Come From?

Yes, I did pay attention in biology so no, that is not what I mean. Rather, I had hoped to present here a family tree but in truth there is relatively little I know about the small number of my relatives. We simply didn't talk much about "the past" when I was growing up and my Mum confirms that this was always the case. I understand that my Uncle Rodney had undertaken a family tree of the Hampsons so I may ask if I can include some of that in an appendix but, for now and in keeping with the original intention to record my thoughts, here is what I think I know!

I was born in Barnoldswick in the North West of England. Barnoldswick was in Yorkshire when I was born there but in a shocking display of ignorance regarding the sensitivities of such things, the authorities later moved the border such that Barnoldswick was included in Lancashire. Wars have been fought over less! It transpires (and I did check) that this travesty of county planning means that I was eligible to play cricket for either Yorkshire or Lancashire, but presumably not both! More importantly, and independent of the county, I am a Northerner and still consider myself such. The North West is still home, especially the hilly bits, no matter where I or my family have moved since. Don't get me wrong, I have loved living in other places and the real "home" is absolutely with the ones you love, but geographically it is "oop North".

Returning to the beginning, Barnoldswick does not have a hospital, so I was born at home in a terraced house on York Street. Needless to say, I have no recollection of this but I do remember being told it so I can state it here with confidence. I already had a big brother, one Keith Donald Hampson who at the grand old age of 4 apparently announced that I was "no use" as I clearly could not play football. I wonder if he has ever changed his mind about that?

Obviously, I also had a Mum and a Dad. Mum had married young (as was very much the norm) at 19 having met Dad at work, he being a much older (as was also the norm) 33. Work was the offices of a factory in Barnoldswick I think, and probably something to do with cloth or printing!

Mum's Side Of The Family

Mum's name is Dorothy Ann Hampson and she is from a small family with no siblings. She was born 10.8.39 and grew up in a terraced house in Earby where she lived with her Mum (Mary Ann Henthorne née Chadwick), her Dad (Donald Henthorne - hence Keith's middle name is Donald, and this before Trump made it popular) and her Mum's parents Elsie and William Chadwick, all of whom were around during my first 10 years.

Her Dad finished school at 14 and went to work on the railways, first in Foulridge and then in Elslack, before moving into Dairy management, first in West Marton and then Barbon in the Yorkshire Dales. As rail work was a reserved occupation, he was excused military service in WWII. He then returned to Earby to work as an engineer at Armoride, a large plastic sheet manufacturer.

There is a connection to North Wales (Rhyll) on Grandad Henthorne's side of the family. His father had a very successful fish and chip shop and Mum fondly remembers her visits there. Grandad had two brothers, Bill and Noel and Mum has a cousin June who still lives that way.

Great Grandma and Grandad were of course a source of fascination to me as a young boy what with them being so old! They may well have been born at the end of the 19th century (born in a previous century no longer has the same caché now that my daughters were) and Grandad took part in the Great War where he was invalided out after service in a tank regiment! Sadly, either I do not remember him talking of his time then or else, as is often the case with veterans, he simply didn't. Apparently, he also went off to South Africa in the 30's when work was scarce at home to try his hand in the diamond mines as a manager, returning home in the 40's. If there is a stash of family diamonds somewhere, we have yet to find it!

My main recollection of Grandma and Grandad Henthorne's house is of a cosy smog! Grandad smoked a pipe, there was an open coal fire and Grandma cooked food to death in a small kitchen off the living room. I'm not sure if anyone else smoked, I think Grandma did. Either way, a blue haze hung over the room and condensation ran down the walls and windows! Grandad liked westerns, both in book and movie form.

The Grandmas liked books of baby pictures. Well, this may not strictly be true but weirdly we were given such by school and told to sell them for charity. They also liked talking about other old people and who had got what illness or had died. They had a pet dog and later (I think) Grandad rescued some budgies! There is a tale of the dog, Peter, being set upon by a vicious Alsatian who ripped open his back causing his death which must've been traumatic!

The other notable feature of the house was a front room for best. This contained drinks cabinets with crystal type glasses and most importantly a piano. We are told that Grandad was a very good pianist and had played the organ at the Blackpool Tower Ballroom. Mum had also learned well but didn't like the practice. Sadly, I have no memory of Grandad actually playing, perhaps he didn't want to if his ability had dropped off. Also sadly, there is no evidence of me inheriting his ability!

It's probably worth mentioning that Mum was brought up as a Wesleyan methodist and went to Sunday school. I don't recall any "religious activity" in the family but it's certainly there in Mum's past. Equally, I'm not entirely sure what defines a Methodist but I'm sure I've asked or googled in the past.

Dad's Side Of The Family

Dad's name is Kenneth Hampson and he is from a small family with one sibling Rodney, although I believe he had a twin sister who was stillborn. He was born 25.5.25 (which is easy to remember) and grew up in Burnley and Barnoldswick where he lived with his Mum (Kathleen Hampson née Hudson) and his Dad (Fred Hampson), both of whom were around during my childhood years. He sadly passed away on 8.3.96 much earlier than expected and far earlier than he should have.

Grandad Hampson came from a large family of 13 siblings (although three died in childhood) of which he didn't speak much, especially not of "black Bob" who inevitably sounds intriguing! Another brother went to America apparently so at least one Hampson in the USA is a relative. Grandad worked as an engineer in the weaving industry and may well be the source of my "sciencey" nature (along with Dad and Keith). Certainly, he had applied maths and engineering books and made things in the shed with a lathe and chisels and so on. Things like ballistas, a pull apart train and puzzles. He did like puzzles and games, especially number puzzles. He was also notoriously tight with money!

I'm sorry to say that Grandma Hampson I know nothing of apart from her salads and triangle rock cakes with jam in the middle. I think she may have had Parkinson's too.

When I was little, Grandma and Grandad lived in what seemed a big (end terrace) house on Rainhall Rocks Road in Barnoldswick. Both were retired and Grandad spent his time in his extensive gardens (fresh peas, gooseberries, strawberries, rhubarb and a wasps nest being my main memories) and the aforementioned shed. The estate was surrounded by a pretty high hedge which we (Keith and I) were occasionally paid to trim when old enough. I believe the rate of pay for the job in the mid 70's was a sixpence each. Sadly, metrication seemed to have passed Grandad by, but I believe Mum and Dad may have topped this up with real money!

I recall we went there often (as indeed we did to our grandparents on Mum's side) and as youngsters it was mostly good fun. Grandad and Dad would also usually host a fireworks session in their garden for Bonfire Night.

Dad's brother, our Uncle Rodney, seemed very different to us then and so we never saw very much of that side of our very small family. I understand that he married a disabled lady who died either in childbirth or soon after, leaving Rodney with our cousin Christopher. He then remarried to Eileen but had no further children with her. It's also fair to say that, since my Dad passed away, Mum has grown much closer to them.

Both Dad and Uncle Rodney were clever enough to go to grammar school but Grandad wouldn't pay and so both ended up going to work on the railways at 14 (or so) with no qualifications. I know that Dad was annoyed by this and I suspect Rodney resented it too. In fact, Rodney ended up working as a porter at Keele University and wrote papers on the Staffordshire potteries (as well as building a huge collection) and I believe he received an honorary degree (tbc) in the end. It is also worth mentioning that he and Dad once blew up Grandma's mixing bowl drying homemade gunpowder in her oven!

Sadly, Uncle Rodney passed away during a lull in writing this and so is no longer with us.

Dad's passions in his 20's were cycling, photography and I rather suspect girls (based solely on his advice to me that I should "play the field" rather than settle down too early!). He was conscripted into the RAF for the later stages of the war where he trained as a navigator and then worked on RADAR stations around the UK (developing a further passion for travel). Clearly Dad had the science/maths skills without being taught them at school.

He got very good at the cycling, winning medals for time trials on his bespoke bikes and touring Europe with a mate on his fixed gear road bike. Just to be clear, this involved touring at least Germany, Austria and Yugoslavia (where they shouldn't have been) after the war, including going over the Alps on a bike with one, high, gear. Ouch! He also learned extensive German whilst he was doing this, specifically "ein ei gekockhte für sechs minuten". At least that's all he ever revealed to me!

His photography was (of necessity) old school and he had the light meters, dark room and enlargers that go with it. An unfortunate legacy of this would be the many painful family shots which required rictus smiles whilst Dad fiddled with settings! Mostly he produced slides rather than prints and looking at photos was an event, the projector brought out, the curtains closed and the screen set up. Tragically whilst he was very ill in his later years, he destroyed the slides so we are missing a treasure trove of memories and a link back to him.

Dad did, however, settle down when he met Mum. They married, had Keith, bought a house (having had to pawn their car and Dad's bikes to Grandad to pay for it!) and had me. Which brings a nice circular conclusion to this little thread. More of Mum, Dad and my as yet unmentioned baby sister to follow.

The Early Years

Not long after I was born, we must have moved from Barnoldswick (in Yorkshire you will recall) to a small town called Hollingworth Lake which is on the North Eastern fringes of Greater Manchester, near Rochdale and Oldham. I believe I have one memory from our time there which was being eaten alive by a huge slavering dog. OK, it turns out it was a very small neighbour's dog but as I was only 2-ish I must've fallen over backwards when it put its paws on my shoulders. Being knocked over and licked felt a lot like being eaten alive.

I remained terrified of dogs for many, many years, in fact until my big brother heroically smacked one on the nose with a string bag full of magazines when it was barking at us on the way to Grandma's!

From visits to Hollingworth Lake since, it looks to be a lovely little place sitting alongside a pretty big lake and with a small fairground/promenade area. I note now (power of Rightmove) there are some pretty grand houses around there too. I can imagine walking on the shingle shore, throwing (later skimming) stones and walking Keith to school along flagstones topping stone walls.

The view to the nearby hills clearly altered as the M62 was constructed on a huge viaduct between two of them. I also recall Mum telling us that the school Keith attended was useless and that the only thing he learned was cross stitch. If this is so, I haven't seen him exercise this particular skill; perhaps the school was so useless he didn't even learn that!

I further surmise that we moved there because Dad got a new and exciting job. Sadly, it didn't last long as I believe he walked out before too long (about 6 weeks). That must've been a huge worry with a young family and a presumably relatively expensive bungalow.

Fortunately, Dad was then able to get a long term job at Armoride in Earby where Grandad worked. More of the job later but I do remember Mum saying this was a difficult time as Dad was commuting from Hollingworth Lake. Apparently, Grandma fed him lunches and Dad put on 2 stone in weight during this time; Grandma's cooking being heroically "solid"! Although, in her defence, Mum has also said Grandma was an excellent baker so maybe it was more the cakes and Northern Puddings that did for him!

So, what with Dad's job and Keith's school it made sense to move back from Hollingworth Lake to Earby, which is pretty much where I spent my childhood. They found and bought a nice 3 bed end terrace with what might be called a courtyard garden enclosed on 3 sides by the house, a wall and the garage where there was also an oil tank and a plum tree. Also, a small border area for plants and, importantly, a footpath running the length of the house to the front where there was a porch and a small front garden. At the back was a lean to "conservatory" containing a trapdoor in which the oil boiler sat. The relevance of these details will become apparent shortly!

The house was, and indeed still is, on Stoney Bank Road. Number 34 if you really want to know. It was perhaps half a mile out of Earby's centre, pretty much uphill all the way. Soon after us the road left houses behind and continued up and then steeply up onto the moors. Across the road was a development of newer houses and later a building site (a future playground for dens and throwing firework "bangers" at my mates) for additional new homes.

Earby was a small town with a railway station and at least two large factories, Armoride and Vokes Filters. The town centre comprised two streets of shops including clothes shops, a minimarket, a TV/Hi-fi shop (you wouldn't find something like that in a town of that size these days), fruit and veg, butchers, newsagent/toy shops and a small sweet shack.

The town had a traditional junior school called Alder Hill where Keith started his remedial education under the strict supervision of Mr Morton (who looked like he was on loan from the Addams family). It also had a very new infant school conveniently close to our home called Springfield and set by a large open space perfect for football, cricket and later golf practice. This lay at the end of Springfield Avenue, a small estate located behind our short row of houses and was my walk to school for the next 3 years and also where my best friend Andrew lived. My other best friend lived in one of the new houses across the road and was helpfully called Mark! We started school on the same day which I think was the basis for our friendship.

One of my earliest clear memories is of feeling desperately sad on the day I had to go to school. The radio was playing what we might now call "easy listening" which was probably the pop station of the time (1967/8) and I still feel sad today when that kind of music is playing somewhere! I presumably liked my home life with Mum and simply did not want to go. Indeed, I'm told that I escaped and took myself back home that same day!!

Of the school I don't have much to say. It was a 1960's liberal affair where there was much emphasis on letting us do what we liked, provided we drank warm milk and had a nap at the allotted times. This can only have been for the benefit of the teachers (who were all ladies) as what 6 year old needs a snooze!? I still don't like warm milk by the way. I do remember spelling tests though so they must have made us do some rote learning and, of course we learned to read at home!

My other main memory of the school was forming my own "gang". Other "gangs" existed so this was definitely a thing. Mine was more of a club really. I made small passports for members with a hand drawn picture of Fred Ted (my teddy bear) so it was clearly a pretty tough bunch. I think there may have been 4 of us. Actually, I do recall being slightly afraid of some kids and bullying was definitely a thing running up and into early senior school. I guess this was a faint awareness of class, there were definitely some "rougher" areas and families and we were all pooled together in the same schools. I do remember having to hit Dad as hard as I could in the tummy when he came home from work once, presumably to toughen up and practice fight skills!

Later I took the smart step of helping the junior school hardman, a lad called Glynn who was taller than everyone else and who did Karate! I do remember him intervening on my behalf at least once. I guess I was always "sporty" but "skinny" so never one of the Alpha Males, as well as being "bright but not too swotty", so kinda got along OK. Which pretty much remains true through to age 30!!!!

Back to the house and its yard. Keith and I found many ways to amuse ourselves there. To start with there was my red pedal car. A concrete garden with a path running beside the house was pretty perfect for it and I loved bombing around there (future love of cars?). Later we would zoom around Springfield Avenue on our scooters, 2 wheels and a brake for Keith, 3 wheels and no control for me! The plum tree made it easy to climb onto the oil tank from where a small step led onto the garage roof. No idea what we did up there, but I do recall going there a lot. Partly for retrieving balls and shuttle cocks lost during sportier moments. The coal bunker and glass lean to both had sloping rooves perfect for improvising ball games which doubtless were the genesis of future tennis and squash abilities. There was also a metal swing in the yard and for a long time I thought I saw it hit by lightning but no-one else has ever mentioned this! Also, the plums were really nice.

Not far from home, across a couple of fields (one of which I recall being an amazing traditional meadow at times, full of spring flowers) was a small playground by a waterfall. A super outdoor spot combining nature and entertainments like slides and rope swings. We went there a lot. The walk was lovely (I guess the grown-ups liked that bit best) and we could splash in the stream and catch small fish in jam jars. Before long we could and did take ourselves there many times. As a family we would also regularly walk down to Grandma's house or drive over to Barnoldswick to see the other Grandparents. I'm told we also did this by steam train sometimes, but I only really remember hearing the whistles from our yard and then being told the railway had been closed down!

Final memory from infant school. Bringing home an enormous Giraffe I made out of cornflake boxes and gummy paper, certainly bigger than me!

The Junior Years

The Infant years over, I then moved to Alder Hill junior school in Earby, just as Keith left it to go to senior school. This was a much longer walk and, as implied by the name, was on top of a a hill, quite a steep one as I recall.

We were equipped with high viz vests for the perilous walk home in winter and I know Mum walked me there at least for a while. There was also a small sweet shack at the bottom of the hill which we'd visit after school and from where, I'm ashamed to admit, I used to nick things. To further assist with walking home safely we were inducted into the Tufty Club. Really can't remember anything about that so I might google it. I assume it was a cuter version of the Green Cross Code man. What do you mean you don't know who the Green Cross Code man was either!? He was Darth Vader. In that Dave Prowse played both roles.

Speaking of walking safely, at some point during this story Keith got hit by a car and badly hurt; I believe concussed. But that's his story not mine and I was blissfully unaware so presumably still small. (He has since told me this was at Hollingworth Lake). Perhaps he wasn't wearing his high viz vest?

Alder Hill was a classic Victorian school, grey stone with separate entrances for Boys and Girls! There was a classroom at each side of the central Hall. Over four years we moved from one room to another until we had completed the set. Each year/room had its own teacher, one of whom (the aforementioned Mr Morton) had been there quite a time! Mr Cross was the Headteacher and he would lead Assembly (or prayers as I think it was called) every morning. He taught when the appointed teacher was missing, otherwise we only saw him when sent to his room for a telling off. I think caning and/or slippering were still in use, but I was never quite that naughty!

Oddly enough, I do remember a phase of collecting broken points from coloured pencils. We started breaking them deliberately and re-sharpening the pencil (in the rotary handled sharpener on teacher's desk) to speed up our collections which we stored in the redundant ink wells in our desks. And when we had enough.... we would flick them at each other! The Playstation Generation knows nothing of fun.

I think it was probably a pretty decent school. There was discipline, we learned our times tables and spellings, we did P.E regularly, art and music and there were "topics" which covered everything else! There were coloured blocks and abacuses for maths and there was endless handwriting practice which clearly did me no good at all. I got told off for reading too much factual stuff and not enough fiction, which was true. Maybe still is!

And there was swimming. Oh dear. Once a week we would get on a coach for the trip to the swimming pool in Skipton, 8 miles away. I couldn't swim when I started. I got travel sick in cars. More so in coaches. Always have, still do! The pool was so full of chlorine there was a haze over the water's surface. Your eyes would melt after a minute and no, of course we didn't have goggles. I was in the non-swimmers group in the shallow end with water wings.

Those who got elevated out of the non-swimmers were rewarded by having to dive in, swim to the bottom to collect bricks, take their pyjamas off in the pool or drown. I'm pretty sure that 4 years later I was still in the non-swimmers group with one other! I hated it and would often be feeling sick before we even got on the coach. I believe this is called anxiety today.

P.E (or games) was a different matter. I enjoyed games. I was uber skinny with knobbly knees and my pumps (plimsolls) were too big for me as I would "grow into them" (sorry Mum but it's true!). This limited my football to dribbling (which I was excellent at) as any attempt to pass or shoot would involve my pump flying off, despite stuffing tissues down the back. I was much better playing football during break when I could wear (out) my pvc school shoes but as this was often 40 a side there wasn't much shooting or long passing required, further enhancing my dribbling.

I loved our version of rounders where, rather than running around a diamond, we ran straight forward to a line and then back again. A boy called Brian and I were the best hitters by miles and were usually on opposite teams. Cue competitive instinct.

Another important activity in the school yard was cycling proficiency. As mentioned earlier, Dad loved cycling and Keith and I were both regularly bought very nice new bikes which we were genuinely very pleased with. I did my cycling proficiency on a blue one with whitewall tyres (sorry Dad, can't remember the make) which came wrapped for Christmas and, as all children's bikes should be, was initially too big for me. Cycling proficiency involved a policeman laying out a road network in the school yard and teaching us road sense.

Staying on was up to us. It was a fine idea and we got an actual metal badge which attached to our bikes when we passed.

Later, I remember Keith getting a "proper" Raleigh road bike for Christmas. It had drop handlebars, a rock hard leather saddle, a 5 gear derailleur and was, er, pink. And I got a smaller proper Puch road bike at the same time. The name confused me for a while as pedal bikes were often called push bikes to distinguish them from motor bikes. I didn't know Puch wasn't pronounced push. Mine had drop handlebars, a soft saddle and 3 speed Sturmey Archer (sun and moon) gears. And it was green. The advantages of the Sturmy Archer gears were several. You could choose a gear whilst stationary. There was no fiddling with a lever on the frame to try and get it into a gear without jumping and no messy oily gears to get your trousers stuck in. We used these bikes quite a lot really and started heading off up Stoney Bank Road to the top, where the moors opened up and took us to exotic places like Gisburn, Keighley and Gargrave.

My other main activity during these years was hanging around the Springfield sports field, both with and without Keith. Basically, we youths would drift there with a football, a cricket bat, some stumps or whatever we had and when enough had gathered we would play football or cricket or lie around. I say sports field, the goalposts were coats. Essentially it was a large, sloping, empty field that the council mowed. Perfect. Later Keith and I used it to get the hang of golf when we purchased a 4 iron and 3 golf balls. A 4 iron might have been the wrong choice for our first club as it was quite long for little me and, as we got better, we could knock our 3 balls quite a long way which involved a lot of going backwards and forwards to recover them.

Tennis started at Springfield too. No, the school didn't have tennis courts, or teach, recommend nor even mention tennis. Sports days involved bean bags and buckets. No, what it did have was a big end wall with a protruding line of shaped bricks at about net height and a decent expanse of grass alongside it. Furthermore, Mum had a tennis racquet from when she was a little girl. It was wooden of course, as everybody's tennis racquets still were. It had "cat gut" strings, as all the best racquets had, although being a bit old they were a little squidgy. The wooden handle did not have tape or anything on it and we were apparently too thick to think about fixing this. Instead, we often got splinters in our hands! But did we spend some hours and days up there smacking a ball against that wall perfecting our groundstrokes. Mostly forehands. And yes, we took turns as we only had the one racquet for quite a while!

What else was life like? Pretty good actually. As mentioned elsewhere, we did very nicely for toys and games, and had a loving home to play them in. I had a small single room where I went to bed with a kind of action man and Fred Ted, and where Dad (who usually came home from work in time to watch The Magic Roundabout with me) would read, or more often make up, a bedtime story. Keith had a bigger room across the landing.

As a family we would play games like monopoly and darts (yup, feathery ones) and my growing collection of matchbox cars would race and jump across the landing. Boys are boisterous so things got broken occasionally (notably a pot giraffe), I told lots of fibs and had a brief kleptomaniac phase so there were plenty of tellings-off too, especially the classic "wait till your Dad gets home". Dad would often tell us to "be a good German" which was somewhat confusing.

Also as a family we would eat at the same time around the dining table, watch the same TV programmes in the evening and have many days out, especially to the coast and into the dales and lakes, passions that remain! The holidays that stand out in my mind are as follows:

Skegness. We went to Skeggy (where it is "so bracing") many times for a summer week. We always stayed in a musty flat. We set off at 4am to beat the traffic which worked as we arrived before anything was open. I believe Skeggy has "gone downhill" since but then it seemed a perfect place for a family holiday. There was a large boating lake, a pool to sail yachts in (I got a fabulous one on one holiday), golf putting (which we played for free in the evening with our own putter), crazy golf, a sun castle with drinks and snacks overlooking the bowls. There was a long promenade with a canal, gardens, a miniature village and the all-important funfair with its "self-drive car motorway". There was an excellent toy shop and equally excellent fish and chips. And, of course, illuminations and fireworks of an evening. Oh, and a large beach, sand dunes, donkeys, donuts. Fabulous donuts. My last trip there was at 18!

Galileos. Mum & Dad had a phase of renting small Transit van based camper vans. These were, very loosely, similar in shape to the Shuttles flying from the USS Enterprise in Star Trek, the main one being called Galileo. So, these became our Galileo holidays. I think it's fair to say we all loved them. Dad got to drive to nice scenery. Mum still had to do all the looking after but she got to see nice places and "play house" in a tiny space. We got to wander, sit, roll, play in the back of a van with no seatbelts. And sleep in sleeping bags up in the pop-up roof! We went to the Southwest at least once (I remember drawing the Clifton Suspension bridge and have been told of ladybird infestations). We also went to Scotland at least once (I remember getting a stagecoach with cowboys) and we definitely made it to John O'Groats.

Caravans. Mum and Dad also had static caravans and tourers at various times, and I am unsure as to which they had when with one or two exceptions! I've heard and seen photos of a caravan in Fishguard which I do not remember, but I do remember the first static at Sand Le Mere on the East coast near Withernsea. It was an Ace something and looked like a stretched tourer! It was parked (sited?) at the back of the site in a grassy field (later ones would be down in the developed area with roads and hard standings – posh eh?). I specifically remember this one for two main reasons. One was rubber band powered gliders and the other was a new member of the family.

My little sister Karen Ann arrived when I was 10 and I lost my bedroom to her, moving in with Keith. She was what I believe is called a happy accident and she may have put a dent in Mum & Dad's plans to be rid of children before too long, although you can hardly hold that against her. Despite being a 10 year old boy I thought she was cute, especially in all-in-one baby rompers, even more so in the outdoorsy ones for winter which were furry. She was essentially an interactive Teddy Bear who could be handed back when messy interaction was needed! We could often be found with me on the floor and she, suspended on my outstretched legs being "boinged" up and down. And she was washed in the small round kitchen sink in the caravan!

I also very much enjoyed pushing her pram (anything with wheels is fine by me) and in particular her "baby buggy" which had limited off road potential and was highly manoeuvrable. Although there is an apocryphal tale of me pushing her ahead on the paths of Flamborough head and towards the cliffs.

The caravan weekends were always great fun, despite having to take a pink travel pill (which tasted so yukky I felt sick before we set off!). Being the worst traveller, I would later get to bag the front passenger seat but initially at least, Keith and I would be bundled into the back seat with Karen in her sleeping bag, er, on the parcel shelf behind us! I think we both enjoyed watching the streetlights pass by.

The Sand le Mere site was an annoying two and a half to three hours away so took all of Friday and Sunday evenings out travelling, although the later opening of the M62 improved matters. We watched the Humber Bridge come into being over the years passing by Hull. The site had a shop, a muddy pool with many pond birds, some sand dunes to shoot at people from, some cliffs, a beach and a very cold stretch of North Sea. Dad would happily swim in this, often heading for Denmark as far as we could tell. Mostly we ran about, dug holes or shivered by the humongous windbreak (a fetching sand colour). Our posh neighbours in the longer caravan next to us had a speedboat too.

On one occasion much later in our story, Keith and I had saved up to buy a two-man inflatable dinghy. Couldn't tell you why but we have both on occasions obsessed about a "thing". Not unreasonably, Dad proposed we use it in the North Sea, presumably so we could accompany him to Denmark. So, one overcast and windy day it was inflated, we climbed aboard and Dad launched us into the first of the series of 6 foot rollers pounding the shore. I immediately found myself sitting on the seabed, no sign of a dinghy, or of air. I retreated to the windbreak to shiver some more.

We also enjoyed the visits to Withernsea just up the road which was a nice little seaside town with an increasingly addictive amusement arcade (boys 14 & 10, first signs of space invaders type machines, c'mon), an excellent bakery and what I still imagine to be the best fish and chips ever.

The Sunday trip home was always enhanced by the fact we came through Skipton half an hour before getting home. We often used to stop at one particular fish & chip shop (there were several) which served Savaloy sausages, Keith's favourite and a Fish Patty which was mine. This was two slabs of potato, with white fish in between, the whole thing battered and deep fried. Add a few chips. Nirvana.

I won't mention them again but I guess we had two or three more static caravans on that site as I remember Keith practicing driving on the small lanes around there so we must have been going there till I was at least 13. I still like at least the idea of a caravan, the bench seats around the front windows, the little dining alcove (also used extensively for card games; cheat's Bridge anyone or a game of Nasties), the rain clattering on the metal roof and the overall feeling that this could be a complete spaceship if you assumed there were rockets on the back as well as gas cylinders on the front.

Before leaving the Junior years, it's worth mentioning that my teeth are terrible, especially anything behind the incisors. I put this down to me not cleaning them properly and the amount of sweets we ate (sorry Mum but it's true!) especially seaside rock. Sadly, my second or adult teeth quickly suffered a similar fate to the first batch; they're as much filling as teeth now to misquote Obi Wan Kenobi. The dentist in Earby was near the shop where Mum worked with Grandma ("Daft Duckworth's" as they called it; I once "won" a football signed by the England team when Mum & Grandma went through all the little sealed tickets till they found the winner!) so I would go over there after I had had my latest extraction. These were done under general anaesthetic, a laughing gas which certainly knocked me out but also made me cry uncontrollably for an hour when I came around. Go figure!

There were also girls beginning to enter my consciousness. Well, one girl. Gillian Preston of "the Prestons". They owned the coal business and a petrol station that would later become the local BMW dealer. You didn't mess with The Prestons.

I, however, did dance with Gillian Preston. The school had some sort of folk dance meets barn dance thing in my final year and we had several weeks of rehearsals. Gillian was tall, girls doing that annoying thing of growing faster than boys at that age, but no taller than me.

Indeed, I was obsessed even then with becoming 6 feet tall as a minimum acceptable height for a male Hampson, whereas my foot size at aged ten was adjudged by Grandma to set a limit of 5 feet 10 on my prospects. I now have a very long neck which I put down to willpower rather than any actual stretching and am 6 feet nothing. Mission accomplished.

Anyhow, as the circle of girls progressed inside the circle of boys, at set intervals we would meet and spin around each other and so, with some careful calculation beforehand, at the big event, I danced with Gillian Preston. For around 5 seconds I should think. It was enough.

By the way, my schools are no longer there. I went back to check and Alder Hill is now a housing estate. There is no sweet shack. Springfield infant school has also been demolished and moved into the sports field opposite, presumably as there is more room for a bigger school but possibly because the one I was in was so shoddily built it probably fell down! Oh, and I might have killed the school guinea pig but that was an accident.

Grammar School

So, onwards to Big School. As this was a long time ago in an England far, far away, pupils were divided into clever and not so clever by an instrument called the 11+ exam. The logic being that the academically gifted would benefit from an education that pushed them harder and set them on a path to University. Those less academically inclined would get more help, progress slower but also get taught useful life skills. The former were called Selective Grammar Schools, the latter Secondary Modern. Subsequent Labour Governments, comprised of people who went to fee paying and therefore selective Public Schools, didn't like this and mostly did away with Grammar schools and selection based on ability. Instead, they called everything Comprehensive schools.

Anyway, the selection process was handled by sitting a pretty comprehensive exam during the last year at Junior school. Alder Hill managed this process well by getting us to sit old papers a few times before springing the real one on us. It occurs to me they could have gone further and not even mentioned that the real one WAS the real one then the kids taking it wouldn't have been stressed at all. And there was stress due to pressure. Some parents would want their kids to go to the "better" school, mine certainly did. Some had siblings already there. I did. Also, there were rumours that the local secondary modern was a bit, er, rough. Heads down toilets, that sort of thing.

I can remember the test had some multiple choice knowledge questions, some fairly easy maths (assuming you find maths easy) and a long "comprehension" test. Tricky.

To everyone's relief I passed, along with most of my friends. Though not all. Mark from across the road didn't and it's interesting how our lives diverged. We stopped being friends within the year. It was expected that Secondary Modern kids would shout abuse at and/or bully the grammar school "swots" who in turn would look down on them from our coach. We must have followed the required stereotypes. Sadly, Mark's life came to an abrupt and tragic end 6 years later when he decapitated himself in a motorbike accident involving a corner and a tree.

Mr Osborne, one of the 3 first year form teachers came to visit the "selected" at Alder Hill to tell us what it was going to be like when we started at Ermysted's Grammar School in September. He pointed out that I would already know because of Keith of course, and that I had a lot to live up to! Now, no disrespect to Keith who was clearly very bright and doing well but that is really not what I wanted to hear. That was divisive and competitive pressure I didn't need. Although I still recall my end of year report which said: "he now has his brother on the run".

The coach picked up from various stops along the route, starting with Kelbrook, via Sough and into Earby where we waited for it outside the ladies' fashion shop. On my first day, one of Keith's contemporaries decided it would be easier to bully me than him and came over to make fun of my briefcase and duffel coat. He then failed to pull the toggles off my duffel coat and to break the lock on my briefcase so in the end it was just a bit of verbal, but I can't say this is what I expected Big School to be like. That said, it didn't happen again so either Keith must have sorted it out or the bully got bored and moved on to someone whose toggles would come off.

Which brings us to another first. Going to school WITH Keith. Well, going to the same school at the same time rather than WITH. I expect Mum thought Keith should take me but there was no way that was happening so I'm sure he walked down and waited with his year 5 (year 11 in today's money) pals and I was with my fellow "sprogs" from Alder Hill including Stuart, Andrew and Brian from my gang. Stuart remained a friend all through school, the others drifting away and leaving at 16 (you could in those days!).

Because Skipton is 8 miles away from Earby, and there were multiple stops along the way, we had to be at the bus stop for 7:30 in the morning. Which meant getting up about 7:00, or sometimes 7:15 (small boys don't need long to get dressed and walk half a mile). I still think of 7:00am as quite early enough thank you and have whinged ever since if I have to get up before that. You may recall me saying I wasn't a good car traveller, and even worse on coaches. Well, I was never actually sick and for most of the first year sat near the front (where "sprogs" were expected to sit) so I could look where we were going and watch the driver to see how he did it. This got progressively harder as we went up through the year groups and further back in the coach which was, in any case, usually heavily steamed up so you couldn't see out. Also, the need for last minute revision meant I had to get somewhat better at controlling my urge to splurge. I loved driving to school in the 6th form!

Now, I think I vaguely recall the coach being a double decker bus early on. We may even have had school caps as part of our uniform too, but I don't think we had to wear them. I recall them being nicked and thrown out the window, which given coach windows don't open makes me think we were in buses for a while! Keith will recall better and I believe he did have to wear a cap…. and shorts for the first year or two. There was much writing and drawing in the condensation on the windows which, if disapproved of by the "Monitors" (Upper 6th formers empowered as Riot Police) would result in them giving the perps "pages" to write. These were harder than "lines" as you had to write something that actually made sense for 2 or 4 pages of A4, as well as do your homework. The "Monitors" amused themselves by thinking up obscure topics like "the sex life of a speck of dust inside a ping pong ball". Two years later, Keith was a monitor. He gave my friend

Andrew pages. Andrew's Dad came calling at the house (!) to have a go at Keith. Keith stood his ground; we were very proud. I lost a friend!

We were in a "house", emulating posh private schools and foretelling Harry Potter. Ours was called Hartley. Inspiring eh? Our school tie (and cap) reflected this with orange stripes and segments respectively. There were 5 other houses. We had "house points" for trying hard and not getting detention (oops) and for sports day. Hartley was rubbish at sports though I've no idea why, perhaps the longer bus journey made us fat and lazy! At the sports day at the end of my first year, Keith and I accumulated over half of our entire House's points (I kid you not), that's how bad they were!

For several years Keith & I honed our golfing skills by cycling over to Barnoldswick where the Rolls Royce Sports and Social Club operated a very pretty par 3 pitch and putt course. We sticky taped 2 or 3 clubs to our cross bars, pocketed a couple of balls each and off we'd go. Not that anyone in the family was a member of Rolls Royce Sports and Social club, or even worked for Rolls Royce. We did this quite a lot, especially in the summer holidays. Pitching onto the green is still by far the best bit of my golfing ability.

Grammar schools were free in that there were no fees, but they didn't come cheap in that the uniform cost plenty, then there was rugby kit (rugby was compulsory), cricket kit (cricket was compulsory), running kit (running was compulsory), geometry sets etc. Then there were the trips ranging from geography field trips to skiing holidays (we didn't do those). In addition, once a year parents would be encouraged to "contribute" to the school's equipment needs. To give some sense of why this mattered, our physics lab had left over bits of Lancaster bombers as part of its electrical equipment. Our uniforms were sized to "grow into!"

After getting over the sheer size of the place (around 500 boys – which reminds me, I don't remember girls waiting at the bus stop in Earby. I wonder where they gathered?), settling in and making new friends, I really liked my time at Ermysted's. For the first few years I found the classes pretty easy and I was usually in the top 5 for most subjects, occasionally top of the class. As a result, Mum would start to ask why I wasn't top of the class all the time and why I hadn't got 100% in a test! In fairness, I did sometimes, er, drift a bit so a bit of pressure may well have been needed. Also, she did help me learn my French vocab every week! Our break times were spent outside, often wandering the grounds or playing ball (on sloping rooves, handy we'd practiced in our yard eh?). I don't recall now what we talked about but we must've talked a lot! Robbo Robinson became my best mate, along with Juddy Judson (imaginative lot eh?), Armpitfred (later Fred, a short boy named Armitstead), Millsy, Helmet and Spam.

A big treat during lunchbreak was to "go downtown". This meant to leave the premises and walk into Skipton town centre, ostensibly to buy something essential but actually to hang around record shops. Until at least the 4th year, a note from your parents was needed to facilitate this. Hence our forgery skills were weaned, and then later refined to get out of Games on miserable days.

Although, recalling trips to town reminds me of a tragedy somewhere around my 4th year I think. Mr Osborne, the same one who had come to visit us in Alder Hill and who had been my form teacher in the first year was stabbed and killed on the school drive when challenging one of the boarders for his permission slip to leave the premises. This was clearly a disturbed individual who was of course removed from the school, but it really shouldn't have happened. Mr Phillip Osborne was, as far as we could tell, a really nice human being.

Our other teachers were the usual mix of characters, some enthusiastic, most cynical and a couple of psychopaths. Chief amongst these was Dai (or Die) Evans, head of physics and deputy headmaster. He would pick pupils up by the lapels and bang them on the wall, he was proper scary. And excellent it transpired when you got to 6th form if you survived that long. The school was long on white boys and short on diversity (there was one Asian boy in the 6th form) and our teachers were very far from PC. This was the 70's after all. Mr Evans taught vectors by reference to "wogs pulling barges in Egypt" and would entertain us with tales of "waking up to find the wogs had shaved you during the night". I think we turned out pretty well balanced all things considered.

I said earlier I was sporty but skinny. Really not built for rugby. Pretty much hated it until as House Captain I had to play again in the 6th form when the weather was nice, I was bigger and I kinda got the rules. Didn't much enjoy cross country running either, so often in driving rain, winds and occasionally snow. My "favourite" run up Forest Lane (a nearby and proper Yorkshire hill) was when we rounded a corner to be faced by a 6 foot snowdrift where the snowplough had given up!

Once a month we'd get to "rotate" into the town sports centre (Sandown) rather than play rugby on its windswept and frosty fields (I still recall the pain of catching a muddy rugby ball with frozen hands!). This was bliss, it was warm and we'd play squash or indoor cricket or climb up wall bars and ropes. After games we would have a half mile dash back to school to get changed before just catching the bus, mostly. Have you tried undoing muddy boot laces with numb fingers against the clock? By the 4th year, we had persuaded a new maths teacher that Basketball was a valid winter sport, and summers were spent playing tennis rather than cricket. I represented the school at both.

By this time, Mum & Dad had sold Stoney Bank Road and moved us to a swanky 3 bed semi with a steeply pitched roof in Sough, just outside of Earby. The house was nice if a bit cold and echo-ey (Mum hated it and thought it was haunted, not least by Romans). But it was right next door to Sough (pronounced Suff) Park which had a tennis court.

Keith and I played tennis there a lot. And by a lot I mean including in light snow (yellow balls a big improvement over white ones here). Clearly, we had our own individual racquets by then and were soon embarked on an arms race to get the latest weapons being used by our heroes at Wimbledon, AMF Head racquets as used by Roscoe Tanner winning out in the end. Thanks again to Mum & Dad for indulging us. Mind you, we were pretty good. I joined Burnley Tennis Club which involved a half hour bus ride each way to play on its six clay courts and where I was disappointed to find there were very few teenage girls playing tennis!

Our tennis peaked with our entry, two consecutive years, into the Ilkley Lawn Tennis Club Open Tournament. A qualifying tournament for Wimbledon. That is, the winner would go into the 2 weeks of playoffs AT Wimbledon to qualify for the actual tournament. So, only 2 steps away from playing on the telly at Wimbledon with our heroes (J.P.McEnroe was always mine). Small point, but being such an opportunity, there were very many, very good (i.e professional) tennis players in attendance. At junior level there were literally coach loads of Mini-Borgs, arriving with headbands and 6 racquets each. Keith and I, er, cycled from home with our prized Head racquet each strung on our backs like some knight of old. It was a long bike ride across the moors which may account for why we were both destroyed in our separate categories. Still, an experience!

The other main memory from our time in Sough was my bike accident. The road from Sough into Earby was an A road and carried a fair number of Tilcon quarry vehicles which were big and scary. One day, I was heading into Earby and just where the kerb was raised stone, a Tilcon Truck came up behind me and suddenly didn't have room to get by, presumably there was a vehicle coming the other way. I felt a shove as the truck hit my back wheel and the bike and I crumpled....onto the raised pavement fortunately as the truck whizzed on by leaving me bleeding (quite a lot). Had I crumpled to the right rather than the left this story would end here.

A nice passerby stopped to ask if they could get an Ambulance and I said no thank you I wasn't far from home. They suggested an ambulance might be a better idea but I got up and pushed/dragged/carried my mangled bike the mile back home. When I went in it became clear why the passerby had thought an Ambulance was in order. Even Mum looked shocked!

To her credit though she did what Mum does and set about calmly patching me up with a bowl of warm water and cotton wool balls. Basically, I had scraped my cheek along the tarmac pavement rubbing lots of skin off and a bit of skin from the bridge of my nose was dangling down where it didn't ought to. Flaps tucked back into place, tweezers were invoked to pick out bits of gravel. They were still appearing weeks later! Knees and elbow took a battering too but nothing like my face. Suitably patched up with savlon applied I then had the face of a gangster for the next 4 weeks "Ooh mister, did you get that in a fight?" being asked of me in a shop in Hull a fortnight later! Hospital? No, Hampsons don't do hospitals unless something has come off.

Keith left Ermysted's in 1977 to head off to Oxford, the second school alumnus to go to Merton College to study physics after Nick Hitchon who was in a BBC documentary! (It was called 7 and it traced the careers of a number of 7 year olds, every seven years.)

In so doing Keith joined the august ranks of Hampsons who went to Oxbridge, including cousin Christopher (Cambridge) and (Dad's) cousin Alwyn, also Cambridge (and who worked at the Atomic Energy Authority in Harwell - see later for more reference to Harwell). He also blazed a path for me.

I used to write letters to Keith once a week and tried to be entertaining and possibly legible. I enjoyed that as a means of still feeling connected. Oxford terms are short at 8 weeks but still it was a wrench him not being around, although it meant I got the double room to myself half the year!

I entered the 4th year a bit of a jack of all trades or polymath if you prefer. I particularly liked languages and was doing well at French, Latin and had just started German. At this point I was intent on being a translator and liked the idea of travel. I was also doing well at science and OK at history and geography. Best not mention handicraft let alone swimming! Oh. You did mention handicraft. OK, a summary. We studied woodwork and metalwork in alternate years. Metalworking resulted in one trip to the nurse with a badly burned hand, an enormous screwdriver and an even more enormous candle holder. Woodwork went the other way, a bookshelf suitable for cassette tapes (or Top Trumps cards), a stool suitable for Karen whilst a toddler and a set of grape cups!

Having largely ignored the first year of German playing chess and/or listening to the radio in the backrow, it became clear I wasn't going to be able to catch up on the basic grammar I'd skipped (word order and endings being whacky in German) so, despite a decent vocabulary this was going nowhere and put paid to my Translator plans. Come O-Levels, I focused on the Sciences; Physics, Chemistry and Biology in addition to the compulsory English (Language and Literature), French and Maths. And I kept Latin going cos I liked it. Fugit ocior aura, ille levi, neque ad haec verba revocantis resistit and all that.

I have passed out (fainted) twice in my life. One of these was in an O-Level biology class. And before you accuse me of wussiness, no, it had nothing to do with dissection (and yes, we still had a rat each to chop up in the lab in those days. Or a frog). In fact, I was the exhibit. Being skinny, my veins were quite easy to see and I had a tourniquet applied to my upper arm so everyone could see the valves in my vein. Teacher then got distracted and when he finally remembered to remove said tourniquet my head received an armful of deoxygenated blood and I fell over unconscious.

In choosing my A-Levels I didn't want to copy Keith but Maths was definitely my strongest subject, so it made sense to add Further Maths to the basic Maths A-Level, in which case Physics is the most closely compatible and besides, I liked it. Plus the compulsory General Studies (which I still think a great idea and should still be compulsory).

Some bonkers friends tried to get me to add Chemistry and do 5 A-Levels but I never really got "Moles" and thought there was a lot more "learning" involved so happily settled for the exact same A-Levels Keith had done. Oops. No matter, I was definitely going to do Maths at University and/or something to do with Computers.

I enjoyed 6th form even more than my time so far. There was a feeling of being treated differently (we would start bumping into teachers in pubs for one thing), we had a 6th form common room with record player and dartboard and a committee to represent the students. Plus, I loved maths and physics and didn't have to do much of anything else. Class sizes were down to 20 for physics and 5 for further maths. Plus a girl for a term but we didn't see her again after that! We also had a French girl speak French to us in general studies. Oo la la. We cared about science and technology and a better future that would be enabled by them. And we learned to drive and got jobs and met in pubs to spend what we'd earned in the jobs. We still wore uniform but with a liberal interpretation; I had a black not grey jumper and a trenchcoat I was very proud of. I was also quite proud of being made House Captain, which meant I got to wear a special tie and Captain the house Cricket and Rugby Teams. Not sure what other responsibilities and rewards it engendered, must've been something!

We moved house again during this time, possibly because of the ghosts. It was a house swap with a slight downsizing so I got a new bike and a Hewlett Packard HP-41C (see the technology chapter) out of the liberated funds. I particularly remember riding my bike a long way during the royal wedding (Charles and Diana) when the roads were fabulously quiet. Wouldn't be like that again until the COVID lockdowns of 2020. The new house was another 3 bed semi on a small estate, this time in Kelbrook a couple of miles from Earby and further away from Skipton and school.

Kelbrook was (and is) a nice little village with a church, a stream, a pub, a garage, an excellent fish & chip shack and a big hill at the back where Dad would often go walking and I would frequently cycle. The house had a small garden with some big fir trees that Dad discovered he was allergic to when he was up a ladder trimming them. We often played mini golf and badminton in the garden and a lot of "revising" was done on the sunny patio, sometimes with eyes open! Importantly, Kelbrook also had a nice little school (infants and Juniors combined this time), still in a Victorian Stone building and this is where Karen went to school. I would often pick her up if I was at home which was lovely. She had her own little (she is 10 years younger remember) friends on the small estate (called Quernmore Drive) where we lived and would often be playing with them. I remember Karen having a couple of issues at the school. First, the teachers refused to pronounce her name Karen with a long a, insisting it was the more common Karen with a short a. Mum was not happy. Also, she got told off for drawing her family as 4 tall people with long legs. When challenged as to who the other 2 (non parents) were, she said her brothers. Teacher pointed out she was wrong (!) as brothers are little like her. "Not mine" she insisted, what with us being 18 and 14 by then! Poor Karen.

On the plus side, we did buy her lots of Mr Men books and probably even read some of them to/with her.

Our house also had a nice view out to the distant hills which is a problem as this meant they were often calling to me/us! We lived here quite a long time, certainly through my University years and Karen's too. Embarrassingly, I don't quite remember when our Grandparents passed away. I know we still visited Grandma and Grandad Henthorne in Earby and I know Karen and Grandad got on really well, but whether Great Grandma and Grandad Chadwick were still around I doubt. And Grandma Hampson in Barnoldswick passed away a long time before Grandad as I know Mum and Dad looked after him quite a while. They once offered to "pool houses" to buy a bigger one so he could move in with us but that was against his financial principles.

Somewhere around now were a couple of touring caravans (one used to move Keith to Oxford) and then another static, this time near Blackpool. I guess Karen spent more time there with Mum & Dad, but I know I sometimes visited after my Saturday job.

Moving to Kelbrook meant an even earlier start for the school bus, especially as they decided to re-route it through Barnoldswick which meant more pickups. On the plus side, there were girls on the bus by now, can't exactly remember when this changed. But I certainly can remember one of them in particular. I was only a 5th year and she was upper 6th but I had my trench coat and steeled myself to sit next to her on the bus and start a conversation. Which went so well we sat together quite often after that. She was gorgeous and I could make her laugh which turns out to be a marvelous thing. At the risk of sounding a bit creepy I still remember how she would neatly fold her jumper and lay it on her smooth skirt. And she wore cowboy boots! Sadly, she invited me to her house for a pyjama party which I wussed out of (what with it being mostly 6th formers going). She gave me a piece of birthday cake on the school bus the following Monday.

Which leads onto the saddest aspect of my 6th form life; no girlfriend. I still don't know why. We all went to the same parties and then most of my mates were hooked up and I wasn't. So, I typically went around with my similarly unattached pals and we concluded we must be the nerdy ones! I did borrow my friend's girl a few times for trips out and even occasional evening drinks and talk. I cycled over to the pub she worked at several evenings to sit at the bar and chat with her whilst drinking manly Guinness. It was 10 miles away. I even borrowed her sister for my 18th birthday party!

Another new thing was music and concerts. Suddenly these were talked about avidly on the school bus along with the latest copy of NME. At the weekends there would be trips to Leeds or Manchester to see the likes of Orchestral Manoeuvres in the Dark or Throbbing Gristle or Siouxsie and the Banshees.

Or Mike Oldfield and Barclay James Harvest if you were me and my mates. Again, getting the feeling we weren't the trendies! My friend Juddy Judson by now was wearing pink PVC trousers with Yeti boots (I quote "it was just so nice taking them off").

Speaking of Stuart (Juddy) Judson, my only trip abroad was courtesy of him inviting me to join him, his Dad and his Dad's new lady in their Morris 1100 on a camping trip to Spain. It was great. We spoke French badly (on the way) and found a skateboard park in Madrid which Stuart rolled down having immediately gone for the highest ramp and fell off.

Another new-found pleasure which has stayed with me for life was driving. I was so lucky that Mum went through loads of different cars! She wanted to learn to drive but mostly was content that she could "get us home" if Dad were poorly. Didn't stop her from trying different cars though. I learned in a Fiat 126 which is like a Fiat 500 but smaller, you kind of slipped it on in the morning. Once I passed my test it was this that I mainly used for driving to school. She also had a number of automatics including a Suzuki Alto with 3 cylinders and 2 gears, a mini, a Fiat Strada (built by robots) and my personal favourite, a DAF 66 with continuously variable transmission. This was red with a silver stripe (Starsky and Hutch anyone), had comfy volvo seats, a huge steering wheel and went quite fast. Witness the missing exhaust pipe after a particularly exuberant humped back bridge. Sorry.

And driving played a part in my job at Harry Garlick's which I also loved. I started at 16 working in the shop. Harry Garlick's was (still is maybe?) a small chain of 4 electrical goods shops owned by a Mr Scothern. I was the Saturday boy and after a properly testing interview (good job I read What Hifi regularly, so I knew my Akai from my Aiwa. Hmm that nerd thing again?) I worked in the shop in Barnoldswick selling stuff in the morning and assembling things in the afternoon. Paid £6 a day.

I worked Saturdays and then holidays too, adding delivery and servicing to my CV once I'd passed my test. By the time I was 18 I had my own vehicle, a stunningly unsexy Vauxhall Chevette Van (that I took my friend's girlfriend out in) and sometimes got to drive the 2.0litre Ford Cortina estate that could spin its wheels in 3rd. While I was there, I persuaded Mr Scothern to stock Video players (VHS, Betamax AND Phillips systems – of which Phillips was the best) and he started renting out films! Also, home computers, the Commodore C16 and C64 being the first we tried. I remember serving one elderly lady who had come in for a portable TV and was adamant about which one she liked the look of. Shame it was a microwave! I did stints covering for staff in the Clitheroe and Earby branches too (though never Skipton) and at the service warehouse. I must have delivered dozens of (large and heavy) TVs, washing machines and Hifis. One unpleasant thing I also did was to retrieve rented TVs (yes, people rented appliances) when the rent was in arrears. Mothers would arrange their kids and their kids' friends in front of the TV so you'd feel horrid unplugging it and carrying it away!

I carried on working at Garlick's through my University vacations and added a pub job for good measure. Those were some long days!

So, finally, what about getting into University? Well, Keith had gone to Merton to study Physics and I had visited him a couple of times and saw that "it was good". But I didn't want to copy him, so as mentioned I decided I would do Maths and/or computing. My first choice was Computing and Electronics at Durham where I could join an all female college that was just starting to admit boys. I figured this would improve my chances of getting a girlfriend without thinking it through. Computing and Electronics?

Anyway, the Headmaster told me this was silly and I should "keep my options open by studying a general course, like Physics. At Oxford where he went. And where Keith went. And where two other Ermysted's boys had recently gone. You know, Merton College". Now, the 1981 year group was described by our teachers as "an unusually bright lot" (that's why I didn't come top all the time, alright Mum?) We had a celebrity in Nick

Hitchon still at Merton, so a "visit" was arranged for a dozen of us. The school had seldom sent more than one or two to Oxford or Cambridge in any given year.

I visited Keble College with one of my mates to learn about Maths as a degree. Pretty much put me off right there! Then we met Nick at the famous Brown's restaurant for a dinner. "Plastic" Colin ordered a bottle of Vodka with no food. He was a bit weird!

So, not Maths then! A good decision as it happens as before long I was really struggling with Further Pure Maths (got a D in the end although that's partly because of hay fever!). So, Physics at Merton it is then. The twelve of us duly applied and most of us got interviews. I went "up" for mine and flunked horribly, I simply didn't understand what they were getting at on one question and the more they tried to help the more confused I got. "How does the light KNOW it's in the slit?"! Hmm, back to Durham maybe. Except that 8 of us had flunked the conditional interviews and decided we'd have a crack at the famous Oxford Entrance Exam.

No-one from Ermysted's had ever done that, it's what the boys from Eton do, not us commoners. Helpfully, Mr Higson (an Oxford MA himself) said he'd help if we got some old papers. A quick trip to Oxford later and we were spending lunchtimes with Mr Higson trying to understand what they were getting at; certainly the questions weren't like A-Levels. Come the day of the exams, we were given the library and the 8 of us got stuck in for 3 hours (various subjects, two of us Physics). And you know what, we did OK and got invited back for another interview. Actually, partly due to lack of expectation, I really enjoyed it, both the exam and the second interview.

Now, if Mum could skip this next bit....we were required to stay over in Oxford in case we were borderline and called to a second interview. So, we were given a room and told to check the noticeboard in the morning. We went out. We met some undergrads who invited us to the bar. I woke up hearing the bells strike 12 noon...so if I had been called for a second interview, I would have missed it! Big oops but didn't happen so all is well and I'm off to Oxford providing I get two E's at A-Level. I think 3 of my mates made it too; as well as the 4 who got conditional offers. We did good!

University

I remember dropping Keith off at Oxford. Mum, Dad and I all went with him in our touring caravan so we could spend a few days "settling him in". On the day we left, I remember him looking very sad and alone. Perhaps he wasn't, but that was my impression. Mind you, I also remember seeing a UFO on the way home and writing to him about it!

As mentioned above, by the time I went 4 years later it was all so much more familiar for me than it had been for Keith. I had Keith's experiences to draw on (and occasionally his work!!), I had visited several times and I had the confidence of the little brother whose big brother has kicked that door down.

So, I reckon Mum and Dad were probably a bit disappointed when they dropped me off. Once more they had taken me down in the caravan and parked up nearby to "settle me in". However, I remember meeting up with Simon (Mills) from school on day one, saying a cheery "bye" and wandering off to "get started"!

Although I had several school colleagues I could stick with (one of whom was at Merton – Andrew Hitchon, studying History and little brother of the TV star Nick Hitchon), I was keen to start afresh so I immediately befriended another Mark who, like me, had been stuck in a disappointingly tiny room in the building called Grove (see above).
A quick explanation is needed re the "disappointment" of my room. I mentioned previously staying overnight at Merton (twice) as part of the interview process. I had stayed in Grove on one of those occasions and had stayed in a very "Oxford" suite of rooms (OK, separate sitting and bedrooms). I was also pretty clear Keith's first year room in Rose Lane was a similar set-up. No, my room was JUST the bedroom, no separate ante-room, lounge, larder or music room, just a tiny bedroom.

In fairness I have learned since that this is a pretty normal situation for students but I was saddened to send Dad away with my record player for which there simply wasn't room! We also enjoyed all the advantages of Merton's venerable age with none of the luxury; lumpy bed, noisy plumbing and one bar fire (google it) for heating. Oh so cold, especially that first January when it hit minus 28 Centigrade IN my room.

The one upside of my little room was that it was on the ground floor so, in Spring, I was able to open my window and explain Thermodynamics to my acolyte squirrel, though I suppose it could be the biscuit crumbs that kept bringing him back rather than the Physics,

Mark and I became close buddies for a while. We were both keen to experience Oxford life, both liked similar music, both keen to get a girlfriend! He was studying French Literature, I think. We also both played darts and enjoyed bars and pubs. Indeed, we played darts for Merton in a league against many other colleges. We were quite good and I spent a fair proportion of my 3 years at Oxford playing or practicing darts, including representing Oxford against Cambridge (no, you don't get a "Blue" for that). OK, it's not quite got the cachet of rowing but there was no way I was getting up at 5am to "break the ice on the river".

Amongst the various places we found outside of Merton that first week were "The Turl", "The Bird and Baby" and "The Wheatsheaf" pubs as well as St Hilda's college bar. The latter being a women only college, we were making progress! "The Turl" is an Oxford Institute, accessed via a narrow snicket off Holywell Street and often featured in Inspector Morse. It was noisy, outdoorsy (in October) and bustling with the clamour of young folk discussing everything – just as Oxford should be! Yes, this was what I had come for.... especially as we were invited back to St Hilda's by two young ladies for coffee and late night nattering. I recall walking back down St Giles in the early morning with Mark and thinking that even the kebab shack was a good idea! Merton was all locked up at night so it's a good thing we'd been issued our keys for the side door into the garden. Yes, colleges still "locked up" at night and there were still rules about overnight guests!

This initial flurry of social activity soon slowed down as it was displaced by the "reality" of being at Oxford, at least the reality for us "Commoners". I could never afford to carry on pubbing at that rate, and really did need more sleep! There were a goodly number of people who could afford to live how they wanted and whose courses permitted them the time to do so! Oxford certainly still had its share of the sons (and daughters) of the privileged who had been to public school and may, or may not, have earned their places through academic ability or Daddy's benefaction. Courses such as PPE (Politics, Philosophy and Economics) allowed plenty of time for Dining Clubs, Rugger and Polo matches and the oh so important networking that would set them on the road to careers in politics and the civil service.

There was little need to eat or drink out, or indeed in your room. We were all signed up for hot buffet style lunches and formal dinners in the dining hall for the whole of the 8 week term and the subsidised cost of this (called "Battels") was automatically deducted from our Grant, aside from occasions when we "signed out". You could have breakfast too but as we have established, I'm not that much of a morning person. Merton's food was famous in Oxford as it had both a decent chef and a huge amount of estate and farm land from which to draw its own produce including "game" for the notorious Game Pie (complete with "shot" and on one occasion an elastoplast).

A brief aside for the younger readers out there, University education was completely free when I went. In addition, we received a means tested Grant for living costs which was, in fact, just about enough to live off, especially given the subsidised meals (and subsidised beer in the college bar).

So, Mum and Dad must have got fed up of not actually seeing me and said their good-byes, leaving me all bushy tailed and excited to get stuck into the Physics. This "settling in week" allowed time for all the fun stuff described above, Rag week of course and the beginnings of study.

There were 8 Physicists at Merton in my year, 6 boys and 2 girls (girls having first been admitted to Merton the year before I arrived so still very much a novelty). There were 4 public school products and 4 state/grammar school types. 2 of the public school chaps had elected to study Physics and Philosophy which is something I should have considered – less maths!!

We met each other and our main tutor Dr Baker where we learned that, along with a packed schedule of morning lectures in the University Science Park, we would have a couple of twice weekly "classes" with Dr Baker (for Physics) and Dr Binney (for Maths) and a weekly tutorial with each of them, either alone or in pairs. We were given some Maths problems to work on before our first class (Second Order differential equations as

I recall, easy for those of us who had done Further Maths A Level, even if we'd done badly!).

We met our second Merton Tutor a little later. A Dr Bowler who was quite a contrast to anything we'd met before. Dr Baker was probably what you'd expect; glasses, Einstein hair, tweed jacket and mustard tie that had been worn so long it was black where his chin rested on it. Also, a nice chap who would try to lead us by the hand through difficult concepts and was nominally responsible for our wellbeing. Dr Bowler wasn't like that.

Dr Bowler wore black jeans, a black suede jacket and a Texan style string tie! Dr Bowler had worked in California with the brilliant and famous physicist Richard P Feynman. Feynman (aside from doing ground-breaking work on Quantum Field Theory) was a professor at Caltech who thought his 2 year undergraduate course should introduce the students to some of the BIG questions of physics, and not just do the rote "simple" stuff (similar to A Level here). I still have his 2 volumes of lectures and they are brilliant. Consequently, Dr Bowler infused with California Hippy ideas and Feynman's enthusiastic genius, didn't care over much for the syllabus or indeed for the drudgery of basic stuff! He would hit us with complex ideas, ludicrously difficult problems and expect us to enjoy them and work out the necessary basic stuff for ourselves. It was not uncommon to go to his tutorial having mastered only one of the set dozen questions! (I learned these evening tutorials went much better if I expressed an interest in, say question 8. He would assume I'd managed the "easy ones" and therefore spend the hour explaining how and why question 8 was so interesting and yet tricky! Others came out in tears. Literally). His lectures (to all 180ish Oxford Physicists) were famous for their enthusiasm and impenetrability. His treatment of electromagnetism started from the point of view of a Martian who knows nothing of magnetism and quickly dived into relativity and the possibility that there is only one (very busy) electron in the entire Universe. Fascinating but this does not come up in the end of year exams!!

I received a book prize for doing especially well in one of Dr Bowler's exams! I need to explain. Often, at the start of term, we would sit down as a Class to do an internal college exam on the previous term's study. Oxford has relatively short terms of 8 weeks with 6 week breaks in between but a lot of work is set for the 6 week break. Dr Bowler had told us to study the first half of the Electromagnetism textbook over Christmas and tested us on this (before the lectures had even started!). And when I say tested us on "this", his questions had very little obvious connection to the content of the textbook. They involved the refraction of light around a distant galaxy for example, a very real phenomenon that is nowhere near the electromagnetism syllabus. Generally, clever physicists scored less than 20% in a Dr Bowler "collection" and mere mortals less than 10%. Indeed, I still recall Stephen Haywood (who went on to become head of a department at CERN!!) scoring 14%. I got 76%.

How? Well, by using initiative. I asked a guy in the year above us if he had any examples of the kind of thing Dr Bowler asked. He provided me with last year's paper. He also provided me with his worked answers as, after everyone has failed miserably, Dr Bowler would then have you work on the problems in slower time with access to books and guidance. Imagine my delight and surprise when our exam paper was unchanged from the previous year! I still have the book I chose, an Encyclopedia with the Merton crest stamped in gold upon it. I refer to it as my initiative prize.

Lest this give the wrong impression, I was not in the upper echelons of academic ability at Oxford, nor even in Merton. I would place myself firmly in the bottom 4 of the 8 of us. Where Dr Bowler could look at a problem and solve it simply by "understanding" what "must" be in the solution and the likes of Stephen would get this, I was in the realm of desperately trying to learn what we were being taught and keep up. I emphasise learning to distinguish it from understanding! It's only really occurred to me much more recently how little I did (and do) understand of Physics and how little I asked "why?" when I was there. In particular my maths inability became a real handicap as we got more advanced. In the end of year 1 exams (which need to be passed to stay on into the second year) I received the "widest spread of results" Dr Baker had ever seen, including an 'S' (for satisfactory) in the Pure Maths paper which is frankly the mark you get for turning up and signing your name. The only reason I didn't have to re-sit was I got an A, an A- and a B+ for the 3 physics papers (and a B-, C and S for the maths). I understand that the Oxford Physics degree now has a compulsory Maths paper in the Final exams, thank goodness I dodged that. Phew!

It was a salutary experience going from "Top of the class" (ish) at school to bottom of the class(ish) at Oxford. Well, perhaps mediocre would be fairer, I'm not stupid! I was around people who were going to go on to do research and PhDs but I quickly decided I wasn't one of them. They could do research, I could (hopefully) pass my exams. So, I enjoyed darts, tennis (I played for the college team where I was complimented on my serve and my bottom in tight white shorts), cycling, evenings chatting about anything and everything, playing games etc. I spent much of my time with my girlfriend Jackie and our friends Simon and Jo, Duncan and Peter the latter 2 of which were with me in the "get a degree and get a job" camp, the former all going on to doctorates.

We once drove to Stansted to see the Space Shuttle on the back of a jumbo jet!

We also did a few "Oxfordy" things like punting, sherry evenings and Sunday roasts with a tutor, going to Winter and Summer Balls and seeing plays/concerts in the gardens, chapels and halls of various colleges. I also did the lighting for a Stranglers concert and one by reggae superstar Desmond Dekker when they performed at Merton.

I may also have spent quite a bit of time later in the evenings spending 10p pieces in the Asteroids and Gravitar Games Machines in a small room near the bar. I got rather good at them which is I suspect is not something I should be proud of given the implications about how much time I might have spent there. One 10p would last me quite a long time by the end!

I enjoyed my time at Oxford. A lot. I love going back there for the unique atmosphere of the parks and colleges, and for the pubs, theatres and museums. I got a "solid second" class BA in Physics which, for the fee of £10 and a ceremony I was later able to convert to an MA (Oxbridge argue that their 3 year course is as packed as most people's 4 year or Masters courses; I suspect others might disagree!). I did this partly because you can but also so that Keith and I could do it together, enabling Mum, Dad and Karen to enjoy a graduation ceremony.

So that's Mark Hampson, MA Hons Oxon don't you know and later, due to a quirk of my work, FInstP which would amuse Stephen no doubt!

I also expect that my education at Oxford at least facilitated me getting the jobs I subsequently had (although Keith had a hand in that too, at least early on) and made me comfortable around very bright and entitled people. Which brings me to my first Prince and only God....

In my 3rd Year, Prince Naruhito of Japan was at Merton studying a Masters (a proper one!) in Medieval Inland Waterways in Europe (having completed a similar study of Japan). Prince Naruhito was the Grandson of Emperor Hirohito, the God Emperor of Japan during the second world war. He is now Emperor Naruhito of Japan. He had a CID bodyguard (complete with bulge under the jacket) and one evening as I was stood at the noticeboard, the two of them walked by. Seemed rude not to say hello so I did, we chatted (mostly the bodyguard) and I invited them into the bar for a drink and a game of darts.

I do wonder whether His Majesty, Naruhito the 126th Emperor of Japan, remembers this?

Work

In this chapter I intend primarily to talk about the places I have worked, the people I have worked with and the things I have worked on. Whilst much of my work has involved "technology", that was often peripheral to the applications and to the nature of what I have personally done, so I have separated the technology into its own chapter which follows on. There is, of course, considerable overlap between these two subjects but I have tried to avoid duplication as much as possible. I recommend you read both for a complete picture of my work life!

Computer Application Developer

South East

In August 1984 I started my career, entering through the doors of one of the offices of Logica, a British company based primarily in London and Surrey with about 1,000 employees and an enviable reputation for quality and innovation. It went on to grow significantly, acquiring 3 large European competitors (and several UK firms) to reach a zenith of around 40,000 employees before in turn being acquired by Canadian company CGI in 2014. During this time, it made a lot of money out of the finance and telecoms sectors and delivered computer solutions across government, transport, industry and, most importantly for me, Space & Defence. I had joined Logica because of its work in these latter sectors, primarily Space, and because much of its Space work was conducted at the European Space Agency in Germany (and the Netherlands). I do not know why I was keen to live and work in Germany but, I was. Perhaps Dad telling us to be "good Germans" when we were little influenced me!

So, I became staff number 6251 of Logica Space and Defence Systems, placed in Communications and Networks Group, Special Systems Division (also known as Secret Squirrels) and my first project was in Great Portland Street London. Hold on, that's not working in Space let alone Germany, nor even at the Mansion in Cobham Surrey which I had been told was my base office! Welcome to the commercial realities of work, I had been placed where there was a need for "fresh blood" to support growth, not where I fancied being!

Also, and as I flesh out in more detail in the Technology Chapter, I had a degree in Physics and my IT skills were pretty limited compared to people who had just completed IT degrees. Somebody smarter than me obviously realized it would be a good idea to broaden my awareness of what Logica actually did for its customers rather than send me off to play at things I thought I knew about. In retrospect, I wish they'd gone a little further and given us some more formal introductory training but the ethos at the time was that if you were numerate and bright you'd pick it up "on the job" (while a customer was paying for your time).

This first project was called DH59 and was classified SECRET. As I had joined Space & Defence, I was cleared for classified work up to Secret, as were all my colleagues. As such I won't say what the application was, but it was for the UK Government Cabinet Office and my job involved testing the system by following various test scripts. Both this, and the application, were quite dull! Less dull was everything being locked away at the end of the day, in filing cabinets with tumbler locks like safes and the warning from the security guy that various people's bins had been searched! It was also cool meeting some of the Logica guys who had been working on other classified systems in West Berlin during the time of the wall.

Commuting to London (from Wimbledon where I lived) in 1984 involved hot crowded trains and tubes and literally dirty air; the cuffs and collars of my shirts turning black during the day, my nostrils going black when walking from Waterloo station to Great Portland Street! I've ended up going to London for long and short stints many times over the years and the air quality has improved hugely, and I think, quite quickly after 1984.

I also discovered that Logica staff drank a lot. Pub trips after work were the norm most days, and lunchtime visits not uncommon. That continued pretty much unabated for the whole of my first year at work.

Next up was a stint at Cobham Park in Surrey, my official base office. This was a stately home with lake, gravel drives, peacocks and parkland bought by the company to be its headquarters. Much more my thing than smelly London! It had a pub across the road called the Plough, fulfilling the apparent need for lunchtime and after work drinking, and was set on the edge of a posh Surrey town complete with a Waitrose (my first experience of posh shopping). My first task here was writing software to enhance a Logica product by the name of LUCID. This was a collection of Image Processing modules that allowed users to load up images (e.g. from aeroplanes or satellites - OK spy photos mostly) and enhance them with things like Edge Detection, changing Map Projection or boosting contrast. This was more like it, there was some maths, some writing of the kind of software I understood plus playing with big magnetic tape reels and doing things to images. I enjoyed that. It turns out the guy I was working for was a world expert in Image Processing which helps!

On that, and as a little aside, in the basement of Cobham park (and in London), some very bright people were working on completely innovative things which we now take for granted. These included Voice Recognition, Word Processing, Databases and in time a complete PC which was manufactured in Swindon. Logica was a pretty leading-edge place to be! It later caused me to wonder how it was that IBM, Microsoft and Oracle went on to take these things to the world whereas Logica eventually sold the ideas or simply dropped them. I believe the answer is the lack of investment from UK investors and/or lack of ambition and business know how. You can add Google, Apple and Amazon to the list of "why aren't they British successes!"

I was then transferred onto a project called RTMC which stands for Real Time Monitoring and Control, the purpose of which was to develop and deliver a computer system to Porton Down to allow them to set up and run experiments safely. As mentioned in the Technology Chapter, here is where I got some much more basic grounding in, and awareness of, what really makes computers tick. Along with the industry need for (and obsession with) endless documentation! This was also a time of making friends, girl friends and playing lots of tennis which was all very nice. And going to pubs a lot! Plus, of course, several visits to the Chemical Defence Establishment at Porton Down.

Portland

My next assignment was to Portland Navy Base, the Admiralty Research Establishment to be precise. Where Keith was! I honestly can't remember how that came about but off I went quite happily. I mean, Dorset is a lovely place to live and explore, Logica paid us lots of expenses and allowances to be there and I got to drive onto an active Naval base every day.

And this when the Navy still had a decent number of ships so there were nearly always one or two in the harbour. There was also a "Wednesday War" in which a ship would set out to sea and be "attacked" by some friendly jets which screamed over the office on their way to attack. Loved it. Also loved the Naval Base refectory which offered hot lunches with stodgy puddings and the fact that Weymouth had 120+ pubs. Logica had a team of about a dozen working on various projects there, all of whom met regularly to socialize (play darts) and occasionally with another Logica team at Yeovil.

I lived in several properties during my time in Dorset including a stint with my brother in Portesham, a house overlooking the harbour in Wyke Regis, a flat in the centre of town and a house down by the causeway to Portland. Also during this time I proposed to my girlfriend Jeanne who said yes!

I ended up staying 3 and a half years, partly because I liked it and partly because I did that foolish thing of making myself useful! I'd planned to go for 2 years, stayed another and then spent the last 6 months actively trying to get out (including going for other job interviews).

What was I doing there? Working on the 2050 Active SONAR system for the Navy's surface ships. It was very cutting edge, the research having been done by one of the other Logica teams working there, along with the ARE people of course. We wrote and tested the software and put it onto the equipment which would be fitted on the ships. What made it very clever was that, apart from being very good at detecting "things", it was also very good at deciding whether the "things" were other ships, wrecks, rocks, whales (known as organics!) or in fact submarines. This was "active SONAR" where the ship puts out a series of loud "Pings" and the echoes are processed by the system (so no operators intently listening to their headphones, that's called passive SONAR). I believe it is still in use on Type 23 Frigates and is only due to be replaced in 2022 (by SONAR 2150). Spoiler alert, this might be the most useful/used bit of software I ever worked on!

Back To Surrey

You'll notice a pattern developing soon in which I spend 2 to 3 years in any given location. Anyway, with the help of the generous site allowances and Logica's "house buying scheme" Jeanne and I bought our first property, a (very nice) one bed flat in Guildford to which I returned once Logica had finally found someone to replace me in Portland.

I then had a particularly "happy time" at work when I both worked on and managed two projects at once! I detail these in the Technology chapter but the gist of it was that Portland wanted me to use my knowledge to do another SONAR project (research this time) but my Boss wanted me to (finally) work on one of his projects which was an Image Processing system for JARIC, the bit of the RAF that handled satellite images. This was all very cool, both projects were SECRET, I had a team of 4 working for me on the SONAR job and 2 on the Imaging job. I was given a company (rental) Ford XR2 due to the regular trips to Portland and Huntingdon and I only broke one of them. Jeanne and I also got married at this time so lots of positive things going on!

As these were coming to a (successful!) conclusion I thought it time to mention that I had joined Logica to do Space work in Germany! My boss said I could do that once I'd done one more thing for his Special Systems Division.

This required going to London for 4 months to design and bid for a TOP SECRET system for MI5 (which I visited several times). This involved getting higher clearance which Mum enjoyed (the chaps doing the background checks are very nice) and some training on tech things I hadn't done before. It was very intense (the Project Manager postponed his honeymoon!) due to tight deadline and very high value if we landed the contract. We did! I designed the software and as far as I know the subsequent project team built it and it was operational for years. I didn't build it because I'd found a customer to ring at the European Space Operations Centre (ESOC) in Darmstadt, Germany and persuaded him that he needed me....

Germany

... and so, in November 1990 I arrived in a dark, wet Darmstadt to a warm, welcoming party! I stayed in one of the very Olde Worlde "Germanic" Hotel Apartments for 2 months while I looked for somewhere permanent for us to live, the plan being for Jeanne to come out in the New Year having rented our flat out. Whilst I had clearly wanted to do this anyway, there was also an element of serendipity, or necessity, about the timing. Having bought our very expensive flat in Guildford a couple of years earlier, the interest rates had ballooned from about 6% to 15% rendering our mortgage unaffordable and introducing us to the concept of negative equity. Joy! Fortunately, as in Portland, Logica paid generous expenses and allowances whilst renting the flat out covered the mortgage. Phew.

ESOC was, of course, a very cool place to be! It was where the European Space Agency (ESA) operated all of its Satellites from. These included Earth Observation Missions, Space Telescopes, Geostationary Communications Satellites and Mars missions amongst others.

There was one large Mission Control Room (very Houston) where tricky activities like launches were managed, and several smaller control rooms dedicated to the individual missions. It was highly international with English the official work language and had all the usual "big institution" benefits like cafeterias and lots of clubs. Logica had a team of about 30 working there full time, as well as people back in the UK supporting other aspects of the work.

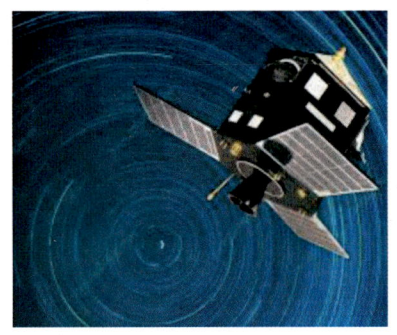

I found my feet by working on the maintenance team looking after the Hipparcos mission (to measure precisely where all the stars are). This allowed me to find out how a Satellite Mission Control System worked and to earn extra money carrying a "beeper" for out of hours support. Must admit, I never really got comfortable doing that. As I lay in bed with it on the bedside cabinet it would "grow" in my imagination becoming terrifying!!

Still, I only got called a few times and seemed to be able to sort most things out, often with the traditional "switch it off and on again" solution!

I quickly moved from this to the reason I'd been brought out which was to oversee and test the work of one of our UK competitors (a company called Science Systems where I end up later!) and to try to persuade the Spacecraft Operators that they should move to a world of Windows with Mice, all very new then. It was fun and went well, despite the luddites protests!

I then got the Big Job that my "reputation" deserved. I say this not out of bigheadedness but because, when I arrived in Darmstadt, I was greeted as some kind of Logica superstar and not because I'd said anything. I can only assume the fact that I'd persuaded the client he needed me and that my last 3 projects had gone well must've been "leaked" in some way. Anyhow, I was tasked with managing the development of a Mission Control System for a new satellite that was being built, the Infrared Space Observatory (ISO). Obviously, I had managed projects before, but only small ones. This time I had a 10 person pan European team (including women for the first time), a difficult customer (like that's unusual) and a brand new (also woman) Logica boss and a lot of work to plan, design, build and test. This was made easier by my best mate at the time (Matt) being the technical lead on the job. He'd been at ESOC for a few years and certainly knew his stuff. It was made harder by the resident "guru" taking a dislike to my "new ways" and influencing a number of the team against me. All very weird and unnecessary and definitely soured my experience of ESOC. Nonetheless, we got the job done and the whole mission was a success, including the bits I wrote!

For most of the two years Jeanne and I lived in a huge, empty, two story apartment in Auerbach which is on the Romantischer Bergstrasse, about 15Km South of Darmstadt and not far from the Rhine. We did eventually put furniture in it, but never enough to fill it, apart from the bedroom which had a giant German bed and enormous wardrobe, both of which caused problems when we shipped them home! This was on the edge of the Odenwald which is a very nice area of hilly countryside and not far from places like Heidelberg. All in all, a very nice place to live. That said, and notwithstanding the problem mentioned above, we were planning to come home after 2 years which many folk did (those who stayed longer than 2 years tended to stay indefinitely) and this was further encouraged by Jeanne falling pregnant and, much more sadly, her father passing away.

South East Again

I think my Secret Squirrels Boss must've given up on me by now! On my return to the UK, I got put on another Space job, working in London on the Satellite Control System for Eutelsat's fleet of communication Satellites. Eutelsat is an organization based in Luxemburg that I've been to a couple of times. During this time Number 1 Daughter, Kathryn was born and we moved to a house in Woking. Always best to change everything at once!

(Incidentally, I went to Luxemburg once on an ESA cricket tour! Not that I was ever much good at cricket, but Luxemburg was pretty! Although, now I recall, Jeanne got horribly sunburned which wasn't so pretty.)

Conveniently my next project was back in Cobham (the newer building this time) and offered a new experience; the properly BIG project. It peaked at around 60 Logica staff and was an overly complex and completely unnecessary (in my opinion) plan to replace the RAF's Low Flying Booking System. The existing "system" involved the pilots ringing up a "chat(up) line" manned by some WAAFs who would look in a ring binder to see if the planned route was free of other bookings. If so, they'd put the new booking in the ring binder in case anyone else tried to book that slot later (for example if a pilot was due to practice low flying through the lake district's valleys, you wouldn't want to "bump into" anyone else). I did some technical work (described in the technology section) as did lots of others. As the RAF has many bases the system was meant to be deployed all over the country and moving maps over the network was all a bit too new at this time! In short, it didn't work and about 40 people were thrown off the project while the bright sparks tried to come up with a better solution. Think it ended up in court.

Whereas my next project definitely ended up in court! This time the idea was a good one; why isn't there a place people can go to see what roadworks are planned so they can coordinate? Maybe the people due to resurface a street could do it just after the gas people have dug it up rather than before! Maybe the water people and the phone people could do their work at the same time? Anyhow, we were supposed to build a system to let councils and utilities share this information on a National Street Works Register. I was responsible for the design of the datatabase (the register) and the software to do the checking and comparing and had a team of 4 or 5 to help implement it. Others worked on the software that would run on workstations that the users would interact with. It all suffered from similar technical issues to the previous project, exacerbated by the councils and utilities all having their own way of doing things and not really being interested in being told to use a national system. Hey ho, kept me employed while Number 2 Daughter Jennifer came along!

And then I ended up working for my boss in a most unexpected and unusual way on a project that had nothing to do with Secret Squirrels. As I was walking across the office one evening, a sales guy looked up and said "Mark, you've done some project management haven't you?". "Yes", said I. "Great, can you go to Kuala Lumpur with me next week?" Now I have to admit, whilst I had heard of Kuala Lumpur I had literally no idea where in the world it was and, as this was before the internet, I went home to look it up in the Atlas!

Malaysia

This was the deal. I was to accompany the Sales guy to Kuala Lumpur (KL) for two weeks. During that time, we would complete the proposal for an airport Network Management Centre. We (well I) would apparently "get the project started" at the same time because it was a "shoo in" and had a tight deadline! In addition, I would get a Sunday afternoon off to be shown around some apartments and KL centre so that I could discuss moving out there with my family for 2 years when I got back!! This was all quite unusual, very exciting and not a bit scary. Jennifer was nearly 1 and Kathryn nearly 3 at this point and my mother-in-law Vera lived with us.

KLCC Twin Towers and KLIA Airport in the jungle

The 2 week stint was intense! My first experience of long-haul business class flying was entirely justified on the basis that, apart from a couple of hours shuteye (on seats that were large and reclined a lot but certainly didn't make flat beds – yet) we worked! I was supposed to land knowing about airport Network Management Centres, about the product Logica was proposing, about our proposal and then get started on the detailed planning and costing. I would also be meeting the local partner (Malaysian IT company called Xybase – the reason the contract was a shoo in), the American Prime Contractor (Hughes corporation) and the Malaysian Transport Minister and his Head of the Airport Project.

On top of this, it was an amazing "project". Malaysia was building an entirely new Airport in a clearing in the jungle and we would have a floor of the operations building (when built!) to integrate all the key airport systems like lighting, baggage handling, security, information etc.

None of this existed yet! The "highlight" of this crazy fortnight was a 36 hour stint in a large meeting room (the sort with microphones on the tables) in which myself and the sales guy represented Logica, along with a guy from our local partner, three representatives of Hughes and their 4 lawyers (I kid you not) and the 3 seniors from the Malaysian airport company once the transport minister had left us. The idea was that between us we would "agree" what EVERYTHING to do with our contract would cost and that included the carpets and toilet flushes per day. Since the Americans had simply been told that they HAD to give us the contract, you can imagine how unkeen they were to agree our prices. Straight through the night we went. Blimey.

I then did another over-nighter to prepare the plans to present to their project manager before I left. This engendered a slightly tearful 4AM of despair when I realized I didn't have the necessary knowledge to do it, followed by a 6AM inspiration to make up a "Time Box" approach to the planning.

During this initial trip we also visited the British High Commission, the head of Tabung Haji Technologies who were bank rolling the project and a few others. My Sunday off allowed me to see a couple of nice expat condo's with swimming pools etc and a Marks & Spencer which enabled me to persuade Jeanne that it would be OK to move the family there for two years!

This is someone jumping off the KLCC towers! I didn't do this but I did see someone fall off whilst it was being built. I also saw several people who died at the airport site. Malaysia had a rather uncaring (indeed degrading) view of its immigrant workforce from Indonesia and Burma (Myanmar).

We didn't get to stay two years in the end as the Malaysians threw Logica out of the country! Basically, Logica wanted paying monthly as had been agreed in the contract but the Malaysians simply didn't work that way. They paid as and when money "became available" and then on a priority basis which could have as much to do with who knew whom and what "leverage" (bribery) had been applied. Logica wasn't prepared to bribe anyone but insisted I find a way to get paid.

I got inventive and managed to get us paid for most of the first 15 months eventually but certainly not monthly. As a result, my boss, his boss and THE Big Cheese from Logica all visited to demand payment despite even the High Commissioner explaining to all of them that it doesn't work that way! I visited the High Commission several times during my stay as this was a "high profile" project. I didn't expect to be back there 15 years later sorting another row (see EASOS later).

I had meetings with the Transport Minister at 1am, I arranged for the Airport authority to visit Manchester (a new airport at the time) to see how it was managed (and watch the cricket while they were there) and a similar trip to Australia, all out of the "allocated" client budget so not costing Logica a penny. In an apocalyptic final meeting, the Malaysian Minister told the Big Cheese of Logica that "they had come down from the trees and won't be spoken to like that anymore" and that "should the Big Cheese visit Malaysia again he would be strip searched at the airport and immediately deported"!

Exciting eh? And you might think that therefore we failed but, no! Having got 12 months' worth of the 15 months money we were owed, I arranged for one key guy to help complete the installation and oversee the integration with the locals at our expense provided the Malaysians agreed to pay for the full contract once everything was complete. He did, they did and Malaysia had the first Total Airport Management System. Logica made a good profit and all 12 of my team got a fabulous experience for 12 to 15 months each and a generous expenses package!

Whilst the airport was still under construction we did get to see completion of the KLCC twin towers which were at that time the tallest buildings in the world. Very impressive they are too! The Logica Office in the City had a good view of them going up.

During that time, unfortunately Jennifer was quite poorly with lung problems and ended up being medevac'd back to the Royal Brompton Hospital in London who continued to oversee her recovery and development for years to come. This was obviously a tricky aspect of being so far from home and indeed Jeanne was incredibly brave staying in hospital with her both in KL and back in London as I couldn't leave. Her Mum was a big help in looking after Kathryn too while I worked stupid hours.

Most tragic of all, my Dad passed away while we were in Malaysia. I got to see him once close to the end and then returned for his funeral. Not great for the family and tragically sad.

On the plus side, Malaysia was very exotic although the ex-pat area we lived in was more like a hot and humid version of America, all very luxurious. There were fabulous swimming pools, trips to cool mountains and white sandy beaches, shopping malls, cinemas, the Tropical Gardens and the jungle! We used to like visiting Bangsar Village which had a nice book shop, a Baskin & Robbins and a Kenny Rogers Chicken Restaurant, as well as much else. We also did the Night Markets, Street Food etc on other occasions. Stayed in some very nice hotels too.

I know this'll annoy Kathryn and Jennifer but...we fit in several bigger trips to Singapore and the islands Tioman, Penang and Pangkor (each with its palm fringed wide sand beaches). For our swansong, we spent 2 weeks exploring the East coast of Australia from Sydney to the Great Barrier Reef before returning home. Being 2 and 4 they don't seem to remember much of this but their passports have the stamps to prove it!

And so, time to go back home. Home? Truly wasn't the same when we got back. I think I got stuck in London again (might even have been the Eutelsat job I mentioned earlier) and our house in Woking seemed tiny after our huge posh apartment in KL (with pool, floodlit tennis courts and maid) and Surrey just seemed so busy and people so rude. Jennifer was much better after her treatment and was now 2 and Kathryn was 4 so we needed to think about schools and day care etc and none of it looked marvelous. Maybe we just couldn't "go back". Or maybe that was just me!

Anyway, having completed yet another two/three year stint of doing different things in a different location I decided to quit (I had been for a job interview towards the end of every two/three year stint but Logica always seemed to come up with something new to do) and because 4 people I knew from Darmstadt worked at Science Systems in the West

Country (well Bristol and Chippenham) I allowed one of them to "put me forward" so he could get the recruitment bounty. All change again, country, house and job!

13 years at Logica completed.

Science Systems And Tetbury

We found a house we liked in Tetbury but my job offer and start date arrived rather sooner than we had managed to move. As Kathryn needed to start school, we decided to move anyway and rent a holiday cottage on a farm with Tamworth pigs for a few weeks. Princess Diana died while we were there which was very big what with Prince Charles living up the road (we saw him close up and said hello a couple of times in Tetbury). TV News crews were a regular sight for the next few weeks. Kathryn started school and we made friends of some of the other expat parents, people like us (aspirational middle class?) who'd moved to the country for a better life.

For the first time I had a job title too, Small Projects and Applications Manager, Science Systems Space Ltd, a division of the Science Systems Group. The company floated on the AIM shortly after I arrived which had no immediate effect but would certainly impact me later!

Shortly after I arrived, my job title became irrelevant! Science Systems Space Ltd had just landed its largest ever project (about £10M) to deliver a Constellation Mission Control System to Eumetsat in Darmstadt who procured and operated Europe's weather satellites. The Managing Director assigned the Operations Director to manage it. Which left their other large contract to develop the Payload Management System for ENVISAT (ESA's huge double decker bus sized environmental monitoring satellite) without senior oversight. So, I got tasked with delivering it. Our contract was for a £4M project delivering to Thomson CSF a French Prime Contractor and involved working with an Italian partner. After about 2 years and many flights to Paris, Rome and nearby Frascati to visit the end customer, it was done!

During which time, the Operations Director got broken by the Eumetsat project. He literally went bird watching on his way to work one day and never came back! So, I got asked to lend a hand to the Project Manager as his Production Manager. Basically, he'd handle the customer and paperwork and I'd get the thing built. They were struggling at the time with a bunch of issues and a disparate team of 50 staff. I guess I must've been quite good at this point cos I got it sorted, largely using jammy donuts as a Friday incentive. Had a few more trips to Darmstadt to visit Eumetsat's very nice building and impressive control room. And sort a few "disagreements" with the client!

So, the "Small Projects and Accounts Manager" had so far worked on the 2 biggest projects Science Systems had! I finally got my "portfolio" of projects and accounts to oversee, and whilst I never again did the technical work, I very much enjoyed having a number of projects report into me, and clients to go and see/negotiate with. This naturally led to more sales and bidding activity and I looked after things like research projects for the UK space agency (or BNSC as it was called then), the work at ESOC and a complex automation project for Eutelsat which we reused for a UK satellite.

This latter activity got me two very nice trips to the Product Conferences of Gensym Inc as we used their Automation product, G2, for our satellite procedure automation. The first was to Barcelona where I got to explore Las Ramblas and the second was to Boston Massachusetts where I got to explore Harvard and where Jeanne joined me to explore the city. We did enjoy that although you won't think so when I say it had a somewhat Anglophobic feel and our accent got us picked on for the duration of the DUKW tour. Oh, and Jeanne discovered she was allergic to the famous Chowder. Otherwise, it was great and we took 2 cuddly black ponies home for the girls!

Most excitingly though, I then got to work with the BEAGLE 2 Mission to Mars.

BEAGLE 2 was the brainchild of one Professor Colin Pillinger of the Open University who had successfully argued with ESA that, as they were going to Mars anyway (Mars

Express) with an orbiter, it would be a good idea to take a Lander along too. ESA agreed but said there was only a small "Mass Budget" available so the whole thing would have to weigh less than 20Kg. Prof Pillinger said that was fine and Astrium (the largest of the UK's several satellite manufacturers) would make it using innovations from UK Universities to make meaningful instruments small enough and light enough to make it worthwhile going. Science Systems won the job to develop the On-Board Software which would operate Beagle autonomously once it was on Martian soil. Unfortunately, it never woke up on Mars having crash-landed!

Beagle became quite a big story while it was being developed with Prof Pillinger becoming something like a household name. Very much a British story of "finding a way" with limited budgets (money and mass). One way of raising interest and funding was to get famous people involved. Damien Hirst created a colour chart which would be used to fine tune the cameras and Alex James of Blur wrote a tune which Beagle would broadcast after landing. I met them both in London and was at the National Space Centre in Leicester for the launch event. There was also an out-reach campaign to go into schools and talk about the UK space sector and going to Mars, with a life-sized model of Beagle. I did a talk at Kathryn and Jennifer's school and don't think I embarrassed them!!

Speaking of Kathryn and Jennifer's school, they had by now moved from Tetbury's "ordinary" school to a private one near Atworth called Stonar which has equestrian facilities. After commuting from Tetbury for a year or two we sold up and moved to Atworth so they wouldn't have to commute, into a lovely barn conversion with a third of an acre and soon after, a big dog. He was a German Hovewart called Hobbes, after the Calvin and Hobbes cartoon.

Then the Managing Director broke! Shortly after he had berated me and 4 other senior members of the Science Systems Space management team for not "stepping up" and grabbing the vacant Ops Director role. He did this whilst drinking flaming Sambuccas at 2am in the hotel bar in Darmstadt! Anyhow, he then had keyhole surgery which went wrong and he was off work for a number of weeks, during which time one of the Non Exec Directors (an ex Logica Director) was co-opted to oversee the Management Meetings.

I got myself "noticed" for having ideas and ended up being promoted to Operations Manager for half of Science Systems Space's projects, me based in Chippenham and the other half being managed by a guy in Bristol. My "management career" had got started!

Businessman

I've no idea what it says about me but, ever since I started work I have had 5 year plans. Where I'd like to be in 5 years' time, what I'd like to be earning and what material gains life would throw up. I therefore started taking a more active role in "getting noticed" by the board of Science Systems from this point on. Before long, a vacancy for Operations Director opened up in the Utilities division of Science Systems. I persuaded the Board of Science Systems that Space didn't need two Operations Managers but One Operations Director and that the other one of us should be the Operations Director of Utilities. I then got a job offer from a tech company in Bath and was offered my choice of roles to stay at Science Systems! And so, I became Operations Director of Science Systems Space, a proper one, listed at Companies House and everything.

Now, Science Systems had been, for some years, two very different businesses organized in 4 divisions : Science Systems Space Ltd, Science Systems Utilities Ltd, Science Systems Industry Ltd and Science Systems Commercial Ltd. The latter of these was as large as the first 3 combined and essentially delivered an accounting product called CODA which was developed and maintained by a different company in Harrogate, Yorkshire. Since the CODA related work was now the largest, and certainly most profitable part of the business, its CEO decided the Science Systems Group should rename and re-organise itself, specifically with a mid-term view to sell the CODA related business and make the major shareholders wealthy. This gave rise to the re-launch of the business as CODASciSys, with the ex-CEO of Science Systems Commerial now Group CEO.

The CODA part of the business bought the CODA company in Harrogate, the SciSys part continued doing the bespoke systems development for Space, Utilities and Industry, now organised as divisions of one Scisys Ltd business. This had the dual advantage of being easier to type than Science Systems and created a larger 400 person business for me to play in! The company also recruited externally to bring in a CEO for the SciSys half of the business.

For the next year or so I was very happy being Operations Director of SciSys Space, albeit no longer an actual director anymore! My pay went up and I started receiving share options in CODASciSys. I became a member of the SciSys Management Team so got to work with the new boss a fair amount and, apart from a couple of weird characteristics I thought he was OK. At this point, my colleagues in SciSys Utilities did me a favour by screwing up massively! The fallout being that the new boss got booted out (!) and my old boss from Space took over SciSys to "steady the ship". And because he knew that I knew what was going on, he made me Operations Director (a proper one again) for the whole of SciSys.

It was about this time that I moved out of the family home in Atworth and lived for a while in a rented flat in Calne before moving to Luckington where I had a cottage in the grounds of a mansion.

I was now responsible for Group Board reporting on all of SciSys's business, and oversaw the big contracts with organisations like ESA, Lockheed Martin, the Environment Agency and so on. I reorganized the SciSys business into smaller, more focused Business Units (Triangles. I've always liked triangular structures!) so as to reduce the likelihood of another screw up. And returned the business to profitability and growth! I suspect this was the most effective I've ever been in my career, I was very good at it.

By now, CODA was doing well too so the big share-holders (primarily the group CEO/Chairman and the CODA CEO) decided to sell up. The problem was that CODASciSys was the registered business so they had to find someone who wanted to buy an Accounting Product business that also did Space work etc. This led to some bonkers conversations where, usually over dinner or in a hotel, I'd have to explain what SciSys did to people who do business finance and accounting. I thought it was really cool that we were involved in sending spacecraft to Mars but weirdly they seemed to think it was a bit risky. So, the board tried to get rid of the SciSys problem by selling it to our main competitor. We didn't like that, and in any case the deal fell through due to greed on the CODASciSys side.

Which left myself and my longest standing colleague thinking we might as well buy SciSys through a management buy-out. Cue trips to "the City" to meet investors and put forward business plans, strategies, returns on investment, exit plans and so on. We ended up with a fully rounded and funded proposal to put to the board. I also ended up with a very jaundiced view of "the City". Bunch of blinkered, selfish, short-termist, misogynistic, racist tw*ts. In fairness I met some less tw*tish individuals later but the short-termist stands! Ever asked yourself why most established British companies are foreign owned? My favourite quote from the evening spent courting investors is "Oh, I see. Well, you seem quite smart, why don't you join us. We just move money around and get rich!". This in response to explaining our plans to grow a business employing over 500 people for the foreseeable future. Needless to say, the greedy tw*ts on the board still thought SciSys was worth more than it was so they rejected our offer!

The new plan was to split the businesses, a de-merger! At this point I was invited to become CEO of SciSys, see it through the de-merger and then lead it onto greatness while the CODA gang got on with selling their business. As I'd just put together a business plan for the next 5 years for the management buy-out, this seemed a good idea, so I said yes.

And there I was, an actual companies house registered CEO of a 400 person IT applications business. I was therefore a proper part of the CODASciSys Board and started attending those meetings regularly, reporting on SciSys. I recruited a CFO, organized my own "Board" and got on with running the company. I also got more share options and another pay rise!

I did two actual businessy things in the next year that I'm proud of.

The first was to take on the large US prime who had decided to kick us off their UK defence contract as they needed some work for their tax friendly office in Belfast to do. So, they decided to give them our work to do! Not sure they expected such a feisty response but I ended up letting them take our £2M (risky) fixed price contract away in exchange for a one-off £300k payment for the "licence" to use what we had developed so far, a £400k compensation payment and a further £300k (risk free) time & materials contract to support them. Very healthy for our bottom line at a slight dent to the top line.

The second was to buy a really good business in Germany. I felt SciSys could grow if it developed more reusable software and products and if it added a more profitable market sector to the existing 3. We found a company in Germany which did some space work which also meant they could handle our German space work for us and provided products and services to the Broadcast sector. I had to go to the BBC to reassure them we wouldn't cock it up as they relied on said products!

The founder (A Herr Professor Doktor Engineer) was ready to sell so many more trips to Germany (Dortmund and Koln this time) followed. There were long meetings with the people we were hoping to buy, their lawyers and customers etc. This was progressing well (and concludes successfully shortly) when....

The CODASciSys de-merger happened. Which left me and my team as the actual board of a listed company. Which in turn meant lots of trips to "the city" to report on profitability, plans etc so they could decide whether or not to buy, or keep, or sell their shares in the business. (Between this, the defunct management buy-out and earlier visits with CODASciSys, I got to know my way around most of the shiny tower blocks and posh meeting places of "the City". Gave my Mum a nice tour once to prove it). As part of the de-merger, SciSys gained a "war chest" with which to deliver an acquisition. Or, at least, that's what I thought it was for...

We got on with business, including big defence contracts with Lockheed Martin to upgrade armoured vehicles, an agreement with Astrium to develop On Board Software for ALL of their satellites, a deal with Arqiva to monitor their network of broadcast antennas through the switch to digital and with the Environment Agency to implement risk-based regulation and inspection across a wide variety of sectors. In addition, I created a new division to look at innovation and productizing some of our projects which is where I felt a growth in profitability would come from.

Oh so hopeful, and on my first tour of The City these plans were well received. But, it was an unfortunate fact that to make sure SciSys looked healthy for the de-merger, these new contracts were big, but risky. And sadly, two of them became difficult and loss making in addition to one of our new managers (recruited by the CODASciSys CEO before the split) decided to hide problems in his area caused by doing the very thing I'd asked him not to do. Hey ho, I was the boss so these things were my responsibility and we had to deliver a profits warning, which inevitably upset our shareholders and made them "wonder" about the new team!

At this point, you need the whole-hearted backing of your chairman and largest shareholder who told me he was right behind me and that we should crack on with the acquisition of the German business before buggering off to the Himalaya for 2 months! In contrast, the EX CEO of Coda who was now sitting fat and happy after the CODA sale told me the shareholders expected to receive the aforementioned war chest as a dividend and that I should then get on and sell the business. Or else. Incidentally, this latter chat took place on a golf course, as did a number of meetings over the previous two years, including a fabulous round at Castle Combe with some big American cheeses from Lockheed Martin.

As I believed in the plan and thought our issues were both understandable and transient, and knowing I had the Chairman's backing, I decided to crack on. We bought the German business and got on with integrating it. As foretold by the EX CEO of CODA, this got me sacked! In fairness they waited until we had completed a redundancy round which had been calculated to correct the profitability issue and had put together a new five year plan. In fact, it was the day I presented our plan to the board that they sacked me. In the evening. Woo hoo. The next day we "negotiated" the terms and that was that, immediate departure for 6 months "garden leave". The Chairman returned for the sacking! By the way, once they sacked me they changed nothing and carried on with my 5 year plan!!

The very next day I went with my new girlfriend Becky to London to visit an art exhibition I had been invited to as CEO, got a bit wasted and nearly met Davina McCall from Big Brother who was hosting the event (weirdly seemed very nervous and also incredibly tiny). In a similar vein I'd previously been to the Royal Albert Hall to eat dinner whilst the "Oldies" (McEnroe and co) played tennis. That was pretty cool.

I was a bit shell shocked in truth and went through the predictable responses of anger, followed by "the world's my oyster" only to end up at "bugger I need a job" after a couple of months. Fortunately, just before getting sacked, I had been due to meet with a colleague from my Logica days in ESOC who was now head of their Space business, a chap called Stuart. He had been interested to talk about acquisition of at least our Space business and was a little surprised to find I'd "gone" when he turned up for the meeting. Anyhow, after a couple of chats he offered me a job working for him back at Logica, looking at potential acquisitions for them, including SciSys! Having a mortgage, kids and now alimony payments to keep up, I gratefully accepted his offer and started work back at Logica, precisely 6 months after my ejection.

So, 10 Years at SciSys completed. Some pretty cool jobs, a few impressive achievements, some CEO hob-nobbing and city stuff and some fabulous send-offs from colleagues who obviously didn't think I should be sacked including a "brightest person I ever worked with" and an "inspiration". Aw.

Logica Take 2

This time I wouldn't be living and working in the South East, my new boss was happy for me to "work from home" and try to create a new Logica Space Business in the West Country (although Logica had offices in Bristol and Gloucester already, they didn't do space work).

I am still grateful for Stuart taking me on when I needed a job, and at a pretty decent salary, but otherwise my next 5 year stint at Logica was mostly a bit of a waste with one exception which I'll come to.

The main problem was that, having been taken on to look at acquisitions, the company suddenly became very cost conscious having just experienced the 2008 financial crash! Stuart still had me look at options and make presentations to his bosses but these all met with a "good idea but not just now". I did at least get to visit a company near Dublin (specifically Malahide, a very pretty seaside town) and another in Rome (where I was taken to dinner by the boss to a very romantic restaurant overlooking the eternal city!) and one in the Netherlands (nice dinner down in the Marina).

I ended up doing a sort of independent sales/account/ideas role. Given the financial clamp down I'm still amazed they didn't "offload" me, which again I suspect was down to Stuart. Mind you, none of us got pay rises for most of that period! One unusual job was to help an entrepreneur who had the idea of a UK privately financed moon lander. It would be paid for by taking sponsors' strands of hair to the moon in a container where their DNA would be safely stored for the time when future civilisations would have the technology to resurrect them! I did some stuff with Skynet which is based in Corsham so "on my patch" and looked at recruiting lots of SciSys people into the Gloucester office which wasn't going to fly without new projects for them to move on to. Which left me helping out on Logica's enormous (£100M) proposal to run the Galileo (Europe's equivalent of GPS) ground segment. The only part of this that I enjoyed was staying at the Police Federation hotel in Cobham. I think I did some stuff in Darmstadt too.

Which leads to the only positive thing during this stint. One day, Stuart asked if I would head up to London to meet with a chap from BNSC who had an "idea". As my role appeared to cover "ideas" this was quite natural so off I trot.

The chap in question went by the name of Ian Gibson and he felt that there was a void in the UK Space Sector. We had great Universities (who along with RALspace have put instruments on nearly every ESA satellite launched), great companies who either made or operated satellites, including some of the largest and most expensive in space and a finance sector that handled funding and insurance. We had a national military capability in Skynet. We also had a government that put a substantial amount of money into ESA

(>£200M PA) but did so by gathering subscriptions from MoD, Met Office, Defra etc. But we didn't have a coordinated approach or indeed a voice.

Ian's initial idea was to create some kind of International Space Innovation Centre (ISIC) at a place called Harwell (where Dad's cousin Alwyn had worked on Nuclear power!) which could provide a focus for discussions around UK Space activity. I was lent to him to help develop this idea and create a business model for it. So, I did. At that time Prof Keith Mason was head of STFC and he too thought this was a good idea and lent his considerable support (in all aspects but crucially in making available the Electron Building). ISIC had a home, albeit a very empty one at that stage as it was simply an office block with dodgy plumbing occupied by We Buy Any Car and one or two other startups.

Diamond Light Source at Harwell; the view from my office window

The plan was for ISIC to be a cooperation between government, industry and academia and it would operate as a club. Government would put in some cash which would be matched by the other members in initial contributions and ongoing membership fees. They would benefit by the resulting growth in Space related activity for the UK sector, with an International outlook from the off. The model was well received and soon government was represented by BNSC and the Technology Strategy Board (which went on to become InnovateUK), industry by Airbus, SSTL, Logica, INMARSAT, Telespazio Vega and RALSpace and academia by STFC, Leicester, Reading and Surrey Universities. The Met Office joined just before everything changed!

Initial match funding of the government money by industry led to the creation of a number of facilities, the echoes of which are still there today. A Satellite Control Facility was built in the Ops room. A variety of different telecoms antennae were placed on the roof and connected to a Comms Lab. A large computing capability was built to handle Climate and Environmental Monitoring from Space which was to be a joint industry/academic capability with a copy in RALSpace and connection to JANET the academic network.

There was a very large videowall, at the time the most pixels in one place anywhere in Europe and for which the National Space Centre in Leicester produced a fabulous UHD video. There was a Security and Resilience Unit looking at classified applications and featuring secure connectivity to government.

And lastly there was my spiritual home, the SPARK room.

This took an idea from Logica to fit out a room as a creative space (hence purple carpets and white leather chairs) with multiple display and input devices where we could engage non-space people and explore how satellites (or satellite technology) could impact their businesses and/or challenges. I also established a Logica Office in the building from which I, and others, could do ISIC work and projects, including designing and building the aforementioned SPARK room and SRU.

This done, ISIC was officially opened by HRH Prince Andrew with whom, I am now ashamed to say, I had a long chat. ISIC now had a seconded staff including me. I was appointed a Non Exec Director of the business, keeping an eye on Logica's investment but also working there.

ISIC was a success. Interest in Space and Satellite Applications was growing. In particular, the Videowall/conference room provided a space where Ministers could come and make announcements and workshops could be held. I met David Willets (minister for Science and Universities) a few times; seemed a decent chap. The SPARK room was where people who would never have considered Satellite as part of their solutions were becoming more aware and exploring possibilities. People, or organisations I met there included Milton Keynes council, the Met Police Chief, the Chair of Lloyds Insurance, Lord Sainsbury, the Royal Security team, people from BP, Network Rail and MI5 again. Oh, and Gerry Anderson of Thunderbirds fame. Also visited and worked with various Universities including Surrey, Reading, Oxford and Belfast.

At the same time, the UK government launched an Innovation Growth Strategy for Space. This too recognised that, whilst the UK was strong in some Space niches, it could be more successful if joined up (building on success in the Aerospace sector). Created with strong input from industry and academia it came up with 16 recommendations including the need for a new Space Agency and something like ISIC with government funding. A new way of doing Space in the UK had arrived and for those of us who had been involved previously this was radical. Since the Thatcher years the UK government had taken a limited interest beyond funding to ESA and pretty much left the industry to get on with it. There was also an agreement to lure ESA to open a Centre in the UK and I was privileged to work with Martin Ditter of ESA to help get that going in the early days in an office above the "Little Stars Nursery" in Harwell. It has since gone on to build itself a shiny new building (still at Harwell) which looks like it's made of Duplo and which now houses the European Centre for Satellite Applications and Telecommunications or ECSAT for short, thank goodness!

At this point, the Technology Strategy Board announced that it too had been looking at ways to grow the UK economy and in particular had been looking at the Fraunhofer model in Germany, where University research had long underpinned industry success. And therefore, it was announcing the creation of a series of Technology Innovation Centres (TICs) in the UK and requested bids from interested consortia.

Clearly ISIC was already trying to do similar things and had a consortium ready to go so, with the appeal of increased and ongoing government funding, a bid team was put together under the inspired leadership of Mr Paul Febvre from Inmarsat. I was seconded into this too, along with a number of other contributors. After 6 months of hard work an enormously detailed proposal was submitted.

And it was successful! TSB declared the winners and Space was amongst the initial tranche. By this time, TSB (which had yet to rebrand itself) decided that TICs weren't a good name (shame I quite like the sound of an ISIC TIC) and so changed it to be Catapults. Recruitment began for the initial team and I was recruited as CINO (Chief Innovation Officer) after some fairly "meaty" interviews!

A little prior to this one very good thing and one very bad thing also occurred. The very good thing was my marriage to Becky on 02.01.2010. The very bad thing was the death of my good friend Steve Ford not so long after our wedding. A lovely man taken way too early.

The Catapult

The early days very much built on the ISIC ideas and engagements, the idea being to accelerate growth in the UK's space sector. The facilities were modified, industry and universities were asked where they thought the priorities should be and we talked to many more non-space organisations to SPARK some ideas.

A large Marine applications conference led, via some complex and extended negotiations to an anti-illegal fishing project which in turn led to the spinout of the Ocean Mind company. Similarly workshops in agritech led ultimately to work with Sainsbury and Colombian Coffee plantations.

Satellite images of open cast mines

A Spark meeting with a senior representative of a global mining company led to a range of projects (particularly in Chile) including the global monitoring of "tailings dams". Other Sustainabability projects came out of a number of discussions with organisations like WWF, Zoological Society of London, UK home and foreign offices, BBC, UN, UKSA, Lockheed Martin, The Met Office and the World Economic Forum which led in turn to UKSA funded programmes including EASOS in Malaysia (See below) and Common Sensing in the Pacific. I was involved in all of these!

As I used to say to new recruits at SciSys when I was CEO there, "Space is Sexy"! This has never been more true than today with private money pouring into new ventures, constellations of new spacecraft providing ever more timely data ever more affordably and a growing awareness that Satellites have a role to play in most walks of life.

Manager/Innovator/Ambassador

As CINO, I undertook a number of functions at the Catapult covered by the heading! It might seem a bit grand going with Ambassador but a large part of my role was to represent both the Catapult and the UK Space Sector to various organisations, at home and abroad. I'll pick out a few highlights here.

The first task was to recruit a team to help me so, in fairly rapid order, I recruited about 20 people to work on sales, marketing, bids and business support/innovation. The TSB (which was now called Innovate UK) had decided that to continue receiving their annual grant, the Catapults would need both to achieve "growth" in our allotted sector but also bring in external revenue to at least match what they gave us. Hence a sales, marketing and bid function. I did quite well at this as over the first 3 years we did indeed grow project revenues to match the grant. I happen to think this was a barmy requirement and led to us bidding for work at ESA and the UK Space Agency (UKSA) against the industry we were supposed to be helping but, hey ho.

During this time some of my more news-worthy activity included:

A trip to Mexico and Colombia on a UK Business Export Initiative led by Deputy Prime Minister Nick Clegg (spoke with him a couple of times, there were only about 20 of us on the trip). The trip was mostly promoting UK construction, education and transport! I was the only one from Catapults so spoke about Innovation a lot and one of only 2 from the Space sector (the other being Professor Sir Martin Sweeting OBE FRS FREng FIET FRAeS, the founder of Surrey Satellites Space Technology). I was mostly on my own surrounded by Colombian government and defence types wanting to know how easy it would be to spy on Peru mostly! We stayed in Bogota (where we had police convoy escort) and Mexico City (smoggiest place I ever landed in) in very swanky hotels and attended evening do's in the Ambassadors' residences where I got on quite well with the head of the Mexican Space Agency. He brought me a nice bottle of wine when he visited Harwell later.

By the way, Business Class flying had got much nicer by now, with seats that lie flat in little cocoons with decent sized TV screens, video on demand and nice dinners. Especially on Air France. Especially on this trip! Although I did break a tooth which wasn't great. I then flew on to Houston for entirely separate discussions with Rice University and the Johnson Space Centre following up a contact my boss had made about the possibility of establishing a presence at the proposed Houston Space Port. We never did much business in Mexico or Houston despite follow up visits, but the Colombian thing became quite big as we ended up helping cannabis plantations switch over to cocoa and helping to prevent illegal mining.

Back in the UK, I went on Network Rail's big yellow survey train out of London Euston to talk about how satellites could help monitor the state of the rail network. Turns out they are continually losing stuff, even trains, but especially copper wire which gets nicked. The train had a meeting room as well as a control room for the survey equipment on board, including a forward scanning LIDAR.

I've also been countless times to London as you might expect including to New Scotland Yard, Lloyd's Insurance (where we met in an old-fashioned board room that had been transferred inside the famous glass and steel building), the Houses of Parliament and related civil service buildings (many times), the Foreign Office (very swanky with paintings, chandeliers etc), Trafalgar House, The Admiralty and several Embassies including Japan, Chile and Australia. But the best one, by far, was the Victorian meeting room on the first floor of the North Tower of Tower Bridge! Who knew?

Then there were trips to Chile. The UKSA got invited to a Space and Defence show there and went with one of my colleagues. The UKSA were so impressed they decided we should go and do some projects with the Chileans they'd met and which they would part fund. So, that's me on a ridiculously long-haul flight to Santiago then. Via Brazil as there were no direct flights! It took 24 hours from leaving home to landing in Santiago where I was collected by a British Embassy driver and taken to my hotel, which was in a swanky modern part of Santiago, lots of glass towers and gardens, very nice. The centre is nice too in a colonial way. The suburbs are a bit more shabby and then there are huge favelas, or shanty towns. I had employed an ex royal naval consultant on contract to "get us" into places and boy did he deliver. We'd usually visit 4 or 6 "potential" customers/partners a day, sometimes accompanied by an Embassy representative.

Over my various visits to Chile, I have visited several mining companies (at Director level) including the state mining operation, the Embassy and Ambassador's residences, the Chilean Transport Minister, the Mining Minister, the Finance Minister and Minister for Education, Innovation and something, all in their swanky offices including the president's palace. Never met the President but she did walk past me at an evening event at the treasury in London.

The Chilean Transport Minister clearly enjoying my visit

Impressive as this is (to me at least) it was the work we did with the Navy that was most surprising. This got me to the Valparaiso Navy Base and their MoD where their Navy people had a row with their Foreign Office people about the work we were doing with them, with us in the room and our Embassy Rep looking quite shocked! Also chased an Admiral to a large Defence Expo 40 miles away to get him to sign off on our contract, that time spent in Malaysia honing my negotiation skills wasn't wasted. Spent an evening attending an embassy do on the flight deck of a Type 45 Destroyer HMS Dragon which was pretty cool. We had a tour of the ship too!

The work we did in Chile was very new. Apart from some stuff on Land use and agriculture, we mainly worked with the mining companies on predicting and detecting dangerous land slips and with the navy on detecting illegal fishing (which turns out to cover human trafficking and drug smuggling too). Think I went to Chile about 4 times including to host and present a conference to a group of government ministries on satellites and applications, plus to try to sell an SSTL satellite to their Air Force. There was a lot of talking through interpreters …. Wait….as I never got beyond basic Spanish …. Wait…. Which is frankly quite tiring….Wait…. especially after a long-haul flight! I once got dragged to meet the local Chambers of Commerce for dinner (huge steak) the evening I'd landed. I got told to slow down as I was gabbling in a caffeine fuelled stupor!!

Bestest visit though was when Becky flew out half-way through to join me. The flights were direct by now though still 14 hours! We did the tourist sites of Santiago, met colleagues for dinner and drinks on top of tower blocks and hired a car to go up into the Andes as well as over to the Pacific coast at Valparaiso and up the coast to Zapallar, a beachy paradise.

Never went to Australia, Canada or South Africa though I did heroically give up chances to do so to members of my team. Did go to the USA a few times though. I'd guess 2 or 3 more trips to Houston to host workshops with the coast guard, city authorities and an International Salvage company with an awesome warehouse full of boats, helicopters and a small submarine. These were mostly done with the UK High Commission (met the Commissioner for dinner) and Rice University, sponsored by another OBE, Dr David Alexander who gave me a reference for my work website! As part of one visit, I got a tour of Houston's Medical Zone, an area of 3 or 4 Hospitals and University departments, huge and hugely impressive, and where I learned about "Pumps and Pipes", a technology collaboration between the health and oil sectors in Houston. Fab. After another workshop I met the last man to stand on the moon, Gene Cernan. Nice chap. (Also met Tim Peake a few times at events in the UK, including at Harwell. Read on for my third astronaut!)

Astronauts Gene Cernan and Tim Peake

Another fun project was developing a Disaster Recovery App for Aid agencies around the world. This was developed with Lockheed Martin (who were looking to get a cuddlier image) for the World Economic Forum (WEF) and got me a trip to the 3 day UN Humanitarian Summit in Istanbul. That was huge, I met various Aid Agency types and Sean Penn (exited one discussion with him) and presented our proto app to the WEF big cheeses.

The conference was opened by President Recip Radogan who looked like a scary mafia boss. Which, by a funny coincidence, is what the "additional" passenger in my taxi looked like. This was because, he was in fact a mafia heavy as my taxi driver explained later, which is why we had taken a slight detour on the way back to my hotel. I was actually quite concerned at one point when we were heading out of the city with this unannounced passenger!!

I did get time (OK made time) to look around Istanbul old city in the sunshine though and it was fabulous. I'd definitely go back although terrorists did blow up the airport the week after I left!

I also went to Washington DC on a couple of occasions, once to present to the World Bank and once to attend a workshop on innovation and finance, presenting how we did it. Also, to drum up funding for our Colombian narcotics operation. Spent the evening at a party hosted by the Spanish embassy.

Back in London, visited the British Museum behind the scenes to talk about monitoring the destruction the Taliban were doing in Iraq. Turns out they don't think anything older than the prophet should exist so were merrily blowing it up or moving it to sell. Also turns out that satellites could tell the museum which without getting their agents shot! Kinda cool being behind the scenes amongst the labs and huge libraries. We did a similar thing for the Security services telling them where stuff might be buried (including Madeline McCann though sadly unsuccessfully in that case).

Continued to meet people at Harwell to show them stuff and talk about what satellites (and the UK industry) could do for them. In particular, and although I hated it at the time, we hosted a series of "cohorts" of senior civil servants who were on a course in Oxford to show them how we did innovation. This included Sparky presentations by me, dinner and drinks.

The attendees included the sort of people who were in charge of building the new Aircraft Carriers and the NHS (the latter leading to some work for us treating strokes in remote areas; oh and that reminds me I hosted a satellites and health workshop at the medical innovation centre in Edinburgh).

I became quite good at explaining and showing what Satellites could be used for. Examples I'd use would include GPS being used to improve train efficiency, spotting a swarm of jellyfish shortly before it bunged up the water cooling intake to a nuclear power station and finding a pirated tanker using Synthetic Aperture RADAR. Also, monitoring land-use, forestry, mining, farming, logistics, security and explaining how innovative use of these could bring huge benefits. Often found myself saying this to foreign dignatories and ministers as well as British ones.

After 3 years of this kind of thing and with the Catapult needing to grow its revenue (see above) I managed a large bid to the UK Space Agency for the Catapult to lead a group of UK industry partners to deliver a pretty awesome satellite/IT system to the Malaysian government. It was called EASOS and in theory we would work in partnership with some 25 Malaysian government departments to give them access to useful and useable earth observation data, initially for flood prediction and monitoring, oil spill detection and monitoring and de-forestation detection and monitoring. Subsequently the system could be expanded to cover a variety of applications. You can see me talk about this on a half hour Malaysian National News channel which broadcast the interview live whilst I was in country to announce the plans. Gulp. Our presentation material was shown to the Malaysian Prime Minister Dr Mahathir.

The good news was that, despite some "issues", OK a "lot of issues" (very few of which were technical!) we got the system built and delivered over the next 2 years. I guess I went back to KL a good half dozen times over this period, usually to be ranted at by various people (including the High Commission – again).

Did some scary big presentations/workshops with incomplete systems in various locations around KL including at the Defence University. I later put the Head of the Defence Forces in the cockpit of a Eurofighter Typhoon at Farnborough which made him happy. I had a go too!

By the way, I've been to Farnborough Airshow at least a dozen times, with Logica, SciSys, ISIC and the Catapult. We've had stands, a mini Spark room, visiting dignatories (British and Foreign) but mostly I liked popping out to watch the noisy jets. Big kid, what can I say!

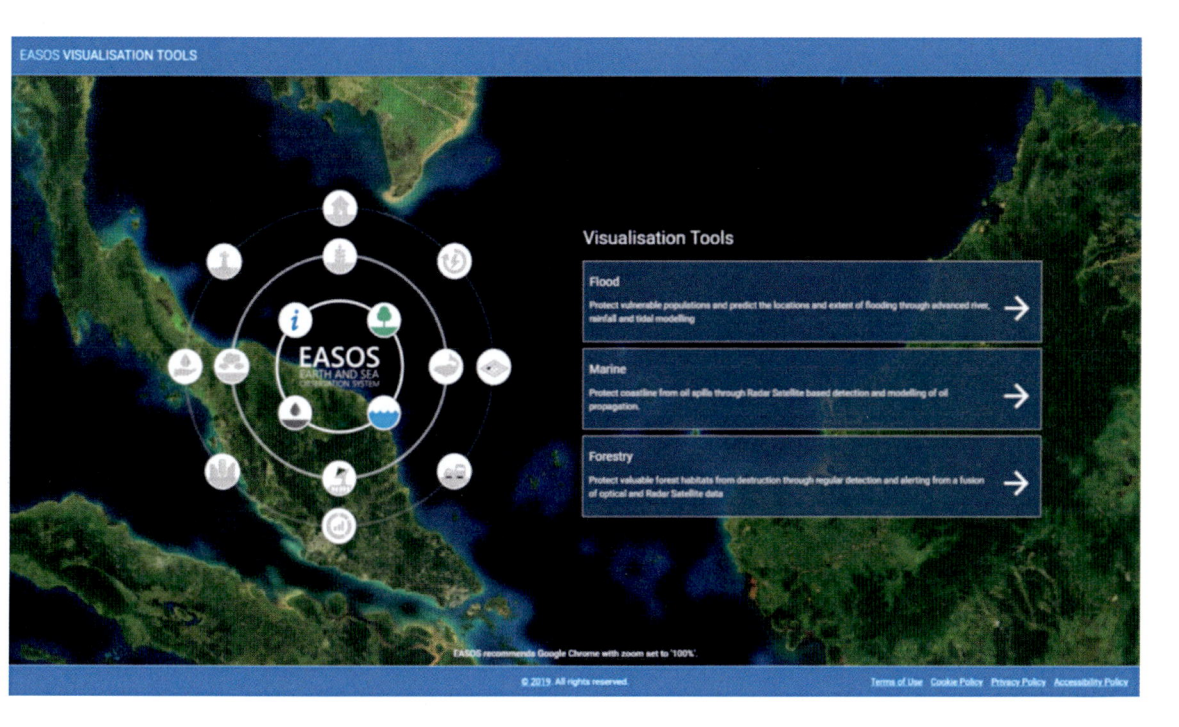

Sadly, politics prevented the EASOS system from being adopted but it was amazing to see it in action. Check out EASOS.ORG.UK where you'll also find my TV interview.

Unfortunately, the project politics pretty much broke me though, what with being called early in the morning by ranting from KL, during the day by ranting from UKSA and our partners and during the evening by ranting from Chile (OK that part only briefly). Still, hit the Catapult's targets and got us all an LTIP payment, and the Catapult team was brilliant. I very much enjoyed working with them (and got some very nice compliments back, like "best boss ever").

I also got a trip to Vegas out of the EASOS work, to the Partner Conference of a supplier we were using, Hexagon Inc. That was cool, stayed in the Venice hotel which really does has a mini-Venice somewhere in the bowels. Amazing place, both hotel and the town.

Moving on from EASOS (although it became a regular part of my presentations) I hosted very many international delegations who visited Harwell. I had detailed discussions with groups from France, Russia, USA, Canada, New Zealand, Australia, Singapore, Thailand, Indonesia, China, India, Nigeria, South Africa, Chile, Mexico, Peru and Colombia. The latter included hosting the Vice President of the country Oscar Naranjo and his entourage!

Also, during this time, I got involved in the Department of Trade and Industry's Export events, including meeting the Global Network of Science and Innovation representatives (all back home from their various embassies where I had visited a few) and presenting the catapult network to 24 MPs in Parliament so that they could represent UK Innovation on their Trade Missions. Helped to foster a putative collaboration between the UK and Australian government's which came to be known as Space Bridge.

At the same time, I got saddled with a fellow director's misbegotten attempts to tap the vast wealth of China. I distinctly remember saying this was a bad idea when it was first announced, but they sent a Catapult person anyway who "opened the door" for a Director to follow up and that Director was me.

There were some positive aspects to this but overall it did nothing for me feeling a bit broken, especially as I was pushed around a circus of "highly diplomatic" meetings with various groups of officials and business men. This included formal lunches where hardly anyone spoke English and it was apparently custom to take turns to stand up and go and say nice words to someone! I was often challenged as to why China could possibly need help from the UK by senior officials, requiring some quick thinking! It was just me and a local Chinese helper who had been assigned to me by a Chinese squillionaire who was hoping we could make him some more money.

The positives were that all the Chinese people I met who weren't being official were very friendly (e.g. dinner with VIP and family), the food was OK for a simple lad from East Lancashire and Chengdu was an attractive, if huge, city. And is where the Pandas live.

The other positive was that I asked to travel via Hong Kong, simply because I wanted to see it! As a bonus, the First Class flight was cheaper than Business Class for some reason so I got to enjoy One Long Haul First Class flight on BA. Woo hoo. Having travelled a lot Business Class and got my "Silver Card" access to fast track and lounges anyway, it wasn't quite as wow as it would otherwise have seemed, certainly not worth the extra money over business class. But still, I wasn't complaining. Indeed, having alighted from my First Class plane, it was a bit of a shock that the flight to Chengdu was out the back of the airport and business class was simply the front row. I was, literally, 4 inches taller than anyone else and the only Westerner on the flight. I did feel very alone at this point.

Anyway, back to the positives! Once back in Hong Kong I had a night and a day to explore before a lovely business class flight home. So, full tourist mode, saw all the sights, climbed to the top of the Rock to look out over the iconic buildings and bustling harbour and it was pretty much exactly like the James Bond movies. I liked! Buzzy nightlife too.

The China thing plodded on another year or so with various delegations visiting Harwell (dinner at Randolph Hotel in Oxford very popular) for big presentations and trips to London. We sent the CFO and my side kick out to sign an agreement (after visiting another Catapult in Glasgow to see what they had done) and none of it led to a single Yuan being "invested".

Not saying I told them so but!

Having been doubly broken, I pretty much decided to leave the Catapult. I'd originally assumed we had all signed up for 5 years or less (we were supposed to take our new knowledge back into industry) but had stayed on to see the EASOS project through and was now close to 7 years.

My last "assignment" was to escort 6 MPs on a jolly, I mean fact finding trip, to the USA to see how they "Do Space" and catch up with a couple of UK businesses there, including One Web. I'm not saying this visit led to the UK Government decision to buy One Web (along with India) but hey, it must have helped. I was there along with industry representatives from Astrium, SSTL and Reaction Engines and we took them to Denver (snow covered airport, snow covered facility out in the sticks!) to see LM and Reaction Engines, and then onto Florida (packed for variable climates!) to visit One Web, Cape Canaveral and US Space Command.

Actually, the visit to Cape Canaveral was pretty cool, we went out to the launchpad where the original Mercury and Gemini Astronauts have their names enshrined and saw the Space-X facility and the VAB. Also met my 3rd and final Astronaut, Bob Cabana in his office, currently director of JFK Space Flight Centre. His previous missions include pilot of 2 Space Shuttle Flights and Commander on another 2 including the first deployment to the ISS. Cool talk plus he has Werner Von Braun's telescope in his office!

So, that's it. There's a possibly more complete and certainly more concise list of cool places I've been and people I've met in the appendix on People and Places. I find it pretty amazing, but then I'm just a simple lad from East Lancashire. You can judge for yourselves.

For the avoidance of doubt, many of these things that I have "done" were "done" with the assistance of many others of course, and many were initiated by others. But I have had a pretty big say in most of them!

Technology

Although my work and technology clearly inter-relate, I decide to present them separately. I have been around the burgeoning IT sector from the relatively early days (recall that there were no Personal Computers or mobile phones or for that matter calculators when I started secondary school) to today's interconnected world so my experience of the evolving kit may be of interest to some. Possibly people who work in museums.

Hewlett Packard HP-41C

Toys

My interest in tech and gadgets started pretty early on. I guess it can be attributed to a Grandad who liked cars and watches (passions which I have inherited) and a Dad and elder brother Keith who liked all things tech too. In particular, a love of science and science fiction kept us all interested in "the future" and Star Trek remains my model for how the world (galaxy?) should work.

Keith and I were always lucky to receive toys that stimulated and maintained our interest. Being 4 years older, Keith would get the "new thing" first, but I often got the "junior' version at the same time and, of course, got to see the "new thing" 4 years before Keith did! In the early days these would include Thunderbirds and Captain Scarlet Dinky toys (and my Mum and Grandma would buy me a matchbox car once per week - I still have 96 of them in 2 travel cases!) with later upgrades to Star Trek and Space 1999.

However, "our" creative needs were stimulated through Meccano sets (metal for Keith, plastic for me!), Airfix models and a particularly fine construction toy called "Playsticks" (or Playstix) which appears to have dropped off the planet. Even Ebay shows no trace (I know because I tried to get some for my brother's birthday recently). The reason I put "our" in quotes is that Keith was always the designer/constructor, my role being closer to destruction testing of his creations. I remain in awe of the occasion I came back from a friend's house where we had been playing with "robot boxers", two plastic pugilists worked by controllers attached to the ring, only to have Keith fashion a working replica from Meccano with pulleys, string, detachable heads and quite clearly no instructions, just my description to work from!

I also recall a chemistry set which did unspeakable damage to the bathroom loo, and an electronics set in which a variety of components were built into a board and could be wired in any number of ways to create circuits enabling a simple radio to be constructed amongst other wonders! We soon cut the components out of the board in order to create more portable devices including (I recall) a radio transmitter to go with the earlier receiver!

During this time, the Meccano also got more sophisticated with light beam sensors, motors, gears and so on. Now "our" constructions moved and caused things to happen (like garage doors opening). I continued to drive my cars around (automated motorways) and shoot things with toy guns but now the things I shot at moved!

(A brief aside, one of my earliest memories is being distraught at the foot of the stairs which I had fallen down, not due to the pain I may have been in, but because I had broken my Sekiden pellet gun. A further cause of distress is that I can remember the make of my toy gun 50 years later but not what I was doing last Tuesday).

Which brings us to the world of computing and programming and the genesis of our careers. Keith also worked in the IT sector. I like to think I led him into it by doing some research in the careers library at school while he was at University, but he probably remembers it as me following him into the same line of work. Indeed, the same company!

In the beginning (i.e when I went to secondary school) there were no electronic calculators let alone home computers. Then, one evening or weekend, Dad brought home from work 4 different electronic calculators, presumably as he had to choose some for work (Dad was chief buyer for the company he worked at). Wow, what marvels were these!! I especially remember that:

1. One had a 3 digit green luminous display! Yes, 3 digits. There was a button you could press to move the display 3 digits to the left or right and an indicator when you needed to do so. Thus, if the answer to a sum were 12,345 you would see 345 on the display and when you pressed the "shift" button you would see the 12, (or vice versa). This may seem madness now but given the display technology was new and presumably expensive, it's not necessarily a daft solution.

2. Another was the creation of the much misunderstood genius that was (Sir) Clive Sinclair before the much misunderstood C5 electric "vehicle". It was tiny, which again given the limitations the day was some achievement. It was black plastic with wobbly studs for keys and had the full eight character LED display so we could write "boobs" upside down on it. (We will return to a later derivation of this little marvel shortly).

3. And there were 2 others I don't remember so well except that I think one of them had a printer roll and big buttons and was therefore presumably much more useful for doing actual "business" stuff on.

By the way, if at this point my sister is feeling left out, I would point out that she was the proud recipient of both a Speak'n'Spell AND a Major Morgan, so plenty of tech there!

I also wonder if I should've covered, or at least mentioned in passing, the use of slide rules and log tables prior to receipt of the aforementioned calculators? Probably not.

Anyway, back to evolution of the Tech. Fairly early on in secondary school I recall that Keith and I both got electronic calculators from Dixons (possibly in Hull close to where the family caravan was located). Mine was blue and did basic maths. Keith's was brown/cream and added scientific functions (an example of me getting the junior version). Both of us were happy and perhaps amongst the earliest in school to possess such marvels (thank you Mum and Dad) and teachers were having to work out whether such things should be allowed. At a similar time, digital watches were also becoming a thing. I've yet to remember the programme but a cool TV character sported a red LED Pulsar watch on a prime time show (on one of the three available channels!) which showed the time when he pressed a button! Now, I think even then we had an early concept of "form over function" as, cool as it was, it wasn't clear how needing both hands to tell the time was better than just one! And so we waited….until the first LCD watches appeared. These too were digital and therefore "of the future" but as they depended on reflected light they were permanently "on" PLUS you could read them in bright daylight (a small backlight made night time clock watching possible too, albeit at the price of needing to press a button). These we had to have and (once again, thank you Mum & Dad) we did. And once again we were amongst the early adopters.

As an aside, thinking of these brings to mind that our Dad who was uneducated (in the sense that he left school at 14 as his father wouldn't allow him or our uncle to go to grammar school even though they qualified; I'm sure his education continued in the real world and especially in the RAF) had a much more nuanced understanding of science and technology than I did then, or possibly have now! Upon looking at my backlit LCD watch he pronounced that, one day TVs would be made of this LCD display technology and would therefore be flat. This in the late 70's when TVs were HUGE (well, our 28" model certainly was). "But TVs are colour", I objected "and require much higher resolution" (I probably said "lots of dots!"). He thought and said "yes, that'll be possible"! Perhaps Keith and I should've got out the electronics kit and Meccano there and then, I can see the name Hampson replacing Samsung in living rooms all around the North West….

Right, enough with the digression, let's return to the focus of this section, how we got into programming. Well, dear reader, this is it, the life changing moment when we first knew what a programme was and that even small devices could be programmed (to be fair we knew of computers and may even have had a basic (!) idea of the BASIC programming language but I'm not sure when this fits in the relative chronology so let's stick to the story).

I said we'd return to Sinclair. Once again, it was small, this time with more conventional (wobbly) buttons and I recall a separate hard plastic clamshell case to keep it safe. It needed this as I'm sure I remember it would re-programme itself or forget parts of the programme if knocked! Certainly, the little LED display would flicker excitingly as it ran its programmes before returning some time later with the required answer to some mathematical problem. Yes, it was only really useful for mathematical formulas but it did have branching and loops - and frankly that's all you need! And the scales were off the eyelids, the world of ever more complex programmes and even more powerful machines to programme was now open to us.

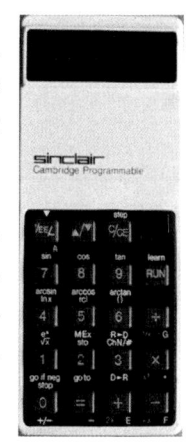

The first major upgrade for Keith was a Texas Instruments TI-58 which added richness to the functions (more conditional tests, more memories etc) but remained entirely numeric. Using this, Keith realised he had all the power he needed for simulation. Imagine if you can (and you had to!) The starship Enterprise hanging in 3-D space, using its sensors to detect the presence of a Klingon warbird controlled by the computer/calculator. The screen would flash out the warbird's position, speed and course relative to you. Was it closing? Where to manoeuvre to intercept and maximise your advantage in attack. Enter a speed and course of your own. Raise shields! Fire phasors and inflict damage as your own shields were impacted in return.... yup, all this from a few numbers on a numeric only digital display. Sounds exciting though doesn't it? And it was.

Next up for me was another leap forward which took me through A-Levels and University. This was the mighty Hewlett-Packard HP-41C (main picture at start of this chapter). This has a super rich "language" with some really quite sophisticated tools (flags, various loop controls, indirect tests) and most importantly an alphanumeric display and string handling. Oh, and a magnetic card reader to allow you to save and load programmes rather than type them in again which was handy as some of those programmes were 300 steps long. I know this as I still have them, both on mag cards and in my bestest 17 year old handwriting! Yes, my trusty HP-41C still works as new (quality manufacturing HP!) 40 years later, provided you can find the slightly weird sized batteries.

Now games like dungeons and dragons were in reach ("oil lamp is running out", "troll ahead you don't have a sword" scrolled across the display) and some meaty stats for making up results from Physics experiments.

By the way, I am amazed that there is a fully functional emulation of this beast available on iPhone complete with Reverse Polish Notation, re-definable keys and fully programmable in the original HP language...

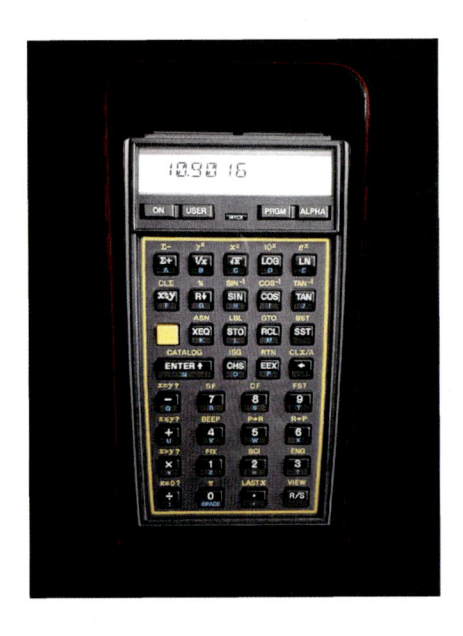

Computers

So much for toys and programmable calculators, it's time to talk about computers. In the late 70's there were many "main-frame" big computers around the world (despite the President of IBM announcing in the 40's that the world would "only ever have a need for about 5"!) used by governments, academia and big business and these would include "super computers" mostly made by Cray and mostly for intensive modelling applications such as weather forecasting.

There were also "mini-computers". The mini here is relative to main-frames which filled rooms. In common with main-frames these had "dumb" terminals which were just a screen and keyboard with no processing capability and were I suspect all monochrome at that point. These were smaller, less powerful computers (albeit packing innovations such as virtual memory), could handle fewer users and so were more affordable. These could be found in most research labs in universities, defence establishments and industry and were where most of my development work would be undertaken.

And then there came the PC or personal computer of which the Founder of DEC (makers of mini-computers) once said "no-one will ever need or want a computer in the home". These were a self-contained computer, capable of running various programmes and their target was homes, schools and offices though probably not in that order.

My story starts with the funky space 1999 looking device shown here, the Commodore (Commodore Business Machines) PET which undoubtedly stood for something as an acronym. You'll note it has an integrated screen and keyboard as well as a cassette tape (another piece of technology confined to the "trash can", although possibly due a revival)

for storing programmes and data. A printer could also be connected, necessary for marking school projects. During my A-level years there were a number of microcomputers (as the early PCs were known before IBM "invented" THE PC in 1981) available to the public. Lurking in my memory are a Tandy TRS-80, a Sharp MZ-80K, a Sinclair ZX-80 and ZX-81 and the PET.

Astonishingly (at least to me) I was entrusted by the school to travel to London to decide which was best. I headed to Tottenham Court Road which was (and is to a lesser extent) a Mecca for all things electric and electronic. So many competing stores on one road and where one could, indeed should, haggle! I selected the PET as the best allrounder and hotfoot back to school to make my recommendation. And that's what we got! I'll be honest, it was hugely popular for Space Invaders and did allow us to do some BASIC programming (self-taught) but we didn't learn a lot. But it did create the idea in our young minds that computers were now available to everyone and would be a huge part of all our futures. My General Studies dissertation was on the impact of computers in society!

At the same time, I persuaded Mr Scothern that people would indeed be wanting home computers and that he should stock them in his stores. This time the Commodore 64 was chosen which did indeed go on to be one of the great home computer/gaming platforms of the 80s. I later had a commodore Plus4 which was a mild tweak with 4 built in packages and I got Dad one for Christmas which led to many grooves being worn in the bedroom carpet (!) - he later upgraded to an Amiga which he loved.

At about this time, Dad got Keith a summer vacation job in the colour laboratory at the Armoride plant where he worked. (Armoride made sheet plastic - remember plastic car seats and vinyl roofs?). The lab was the proud owner of a new mini-computer for pigment analysis and colour matching and was called (I think - though this is more Keith's story) an ICS. What I do recall is that it was programmed in BASICS (an ICS variant on BASIC presumably) which allowed us to programme it to play minehunter! There is an apocryphal tale from Mum of Keith "breaking" said computer and Dad being very cross. Like I say, not my story! But my first experience of a "proper" computer with a teletype.

And so, to University where the computer pickings were surprisingly slim. There in the labs we were introduced to the Research Machines 380Z which apart from sounding like a popular Nissan sports coupe of the time had nothing going for it. We were required to use it for processing results of experiments doing things like least squares fits on the data.

Fast forward to the world of work and professional software development. My first taste of this was a summer vacation job at the end of the second year when I did a 6 week stint at a branch of the mighty GEC empire called EASAMS in Camberley, Surrey. Now, if you recall the introduction, I had done some research in the school careers library in the 6th form in which I had discovered there was such a thing as a career in computing and that the BIG 4 at the time were Software Sciences, Logica, Scicon and CAP. EASAMS also made my list as they did cool defence stuff. I expect others were available. You will also recall that I believe this research informed and led my brother into his choices being the same as mine and that therefore it won't surprise you to know that EASAMS was where Keith was working at this time! I can only assume, in retrospect, that either he had a hand in getting me my first two jobs or at the very least he must have made a good impression as they didn't seem to mind getting another Hampson.

At EASAMS I learned a lot about what a modern IT development business was like. There were bright graduates developing missile guidance software and stuff for submarines, aircraft and so on. They drank a lot. Unlike students, they could afford to drink a lot. Most importantly, their development computer was a Control Data Corporation CDC Cyber 171 which is a really cool name for a computer. It was water cooled (yup, really) AND it was kept in an air conditioned basement, the only air conditioned part of the office so getting "time" on the console was a precious and cooling thing that hot summer! And what, was I doing there? Well, one for the IT nerds this, I was building a database of re-useable code modules so the real programmers wouldn't keep re-inventing the wheel! An early, in house software library. I have no idea whether it was useful but it was an interesting project with an actual outcome and I got to learn about databases so certainly did me no harm. If not my liver!

So, the first proper job was at Logica where Keith worked (having moved from EASAMS)! Now, in a desperate attempt to not follow Keith into the company that I had chosen, I had applied for jobs at:

- Logica because it did Space work in Germany,

- EASAMS as it seemed a banker after the summer job,

- Marks & Spencer because it paid more and their headquarters was almost entirely staffed by women and

- BP to do Geophysics (either on computers or out in the field).

BP offered me a job but I decided I wasn't actually robust enough to go around well logging in jungles and deserts. M&S offered me a job and then changed their mind about having an in house IT team and decided to outsource instead. It's an interesting "what if" had they not done this as I had been tempted by the call of the higher pay and the free nail jobs. Which left EASAMS and Logica and … Logica did space work in Germany. I really wanted to go to Germany although I couldn't tell you why!

I did some pretty cool projects at Logica which are described in the Work chapter. Here I encountered my first DEC VAX 11/750 in the basement of Cobham Park on which I wrote some "primitives" (simple routines) for Logica's LUCID image processing product. These were written in FORTRAN I believe and did things like edge detection and map projections for Earth Observation imagery (OK spy satellites). Next, I was most miffed as I had joined Logica to do space work in Germany (I may have mentioned this) but had been placed in the Special Systems Division of Secure Networks Group in the Defence (and Intelligence) bit of Logica Space & Defence. Secure Networks? No rockets there. But somebody smarter than me had realised that whilst I knew about physics and could write some programmes, I didn't actually know much about computers. Let me explain…

I was interviewed by the Project Manager of a project called RTMC to join his team. He asked about my experience. He said they needed someone to write a screen editor. I said "eh?" or something more professional but amounting to the same thing. "What do you mean, write a screen editor?" "Well," he wisely explained, "an editor is a programme, just like a compiler". "What, I thought things like that simply came with the computer, they always seem to have them?". "Well," he patiently explained, "that's because someone has written the code for them". "OK", I say, slowly cottoning on," but how do you write a screen editor without….an editor?". "OK," he says, "that's a better question, you use a line editor". So, warming to my task I ask "why the heck have you bought a computer that doesn't have an editor already?" Losing patience, and because he doubtless had many meetings to attend (as I learned later in my career), he explained "because these stripped down machines are the only ones quick enough for what we are doing". OK. So, I wrote a screen editor in PASCAL for a Computer Automations computer which ran the bespoke CARTOS operating system. This apparently stood for Computer Automations Real Time Operating System but we had such trouble getting it to move quickly we re-christened it Cart'Orse. The remainder of my education on this project came from the fact that one chap was developing a compiler for the bespoke language we were creating and another was programming the target microprocessors in Assembler.

Newly wise I headed to my next assignment, to the Admiralty Research Establishment on Portland, where my brother worked! Honestly can't remember how this came about and it was the last, and closest, time our careers overlapped. The appeal for me was working on defencey stuff and that, at that time, Logica paid generous site allowances and expenses. The application this time was operationalising research into active SONAR processing to produce a working version to go to sea with the navy as the 2016 and later 2050 SONAR suites. More on my time in Dorset appears elsewhere, here the tech elements comprised initially a DEC PDP 11/45 and then 11/70. These were minicomputers of their time and actually a step back from the VAX used at Logica. That said, instead of threading tapes onto tape drives as I had at Logica, I could now load external disks into things the size of top loading washing machines! Weirdly, both activities made me feel very Hollywood. Go figure! As for the PDPs themselves, I'm not sure what the operating system was but they had "DIP" switches on the front which had to be set to the correct settings before "booting" the computer up. Also, weirdly cool.

I think I'd like to do something similar before firing up my laptop. Or car. Perhaps it's that jet fighter association of checking lots of dials and switches before starting up. Perhaps it's just me! Other exciting equipment we had in the lab included a RAMTEK raster display (worked superbly for a FORTRAN version of "moonlander") and the OLPARS neural network emulator. Please note, mid 1980s neural network, these ideas have been around a while! It was used for pattern recognition. Where the PDP was used for research (mostly by other teams), we developed the operational software on a VAX 11/750 for deployment onto an array of Ferranti M700 processors (M for Military) via an Argus 700. The code was developed on the VAX in CORAL 66. This is not a language most of you will have heard of, but the joke even at the time was "Coral code found in Viking village". Cutting edge it wasn't! That said, it was much like PASCAL and made embedding machine code very easy 'CODE BEGIN'....'CODE END' which was important for the real time bits like the Fast Fourier transforms.

Furthermore, this was where I first encountered....colour monitors! Still dumb, but made editing easier by assigning different colours to constructs, keywords, comments etc. More importantly, it meant that you could code entirely in red on a Friday afternoon after 2 hours at the pub....

And the operational displays looked something like this. A different team wrote the MMI (as it was known then, before the more pc HMI came into fashion!) but I often enjoyed demoing the system on these. Except the time our boss dragged his tie across the sensitive touch panels during an important demo and sent the system crazy. Navy operators do not wear ties when operating such systems. As a group, this team at the ARE were world leading at submarine detection and classification and I was proud to be a small part of the group.

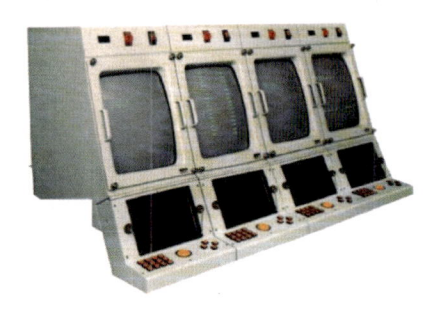

Three and a half years later I left Dorset and returned to the Mothership in Cobham, Surrey where Logica now had two offices, the stately home of Cobham Park (complete with Peacocks, gravel drives and a lake) and a new funky modern building in the centre of the village. I didn't entirely escape Portland as one of the bosses there was keen that we should use our knowledge of 2016/2050 to look at the data from an active dipping SONAR bistatic trial. This was fine but my boss (Intelligence or secret squirrels as we usually referred to it) wanted me to start working for him after 5 years working for others! This led to, what is in retrospect, one of the happiest work periods I ever had at the tech coal face.

I was able to build a small team (of 5) in the basement of Cobham Park to undertake the bistatic SONAR work and, at the same time, I had a team (of 2) work for me in a different basement room along the corridor. So, I was Project Manager of 2 projects at once, both were classified secret, both teams were fun and the tech was cool. As I shall explain...

The SONAR work was carried out on a dedicated VAX again but this time in Ada. Ada was and remains my favourite programming language. We didn't really need to tap its Object Oriented aspects but for shear readability and error handling it was a pleasure. The data now came on VHS cassettes and we had an actual PC for doing project reporting and playing golf. With a removable hard drive to lock away at night in case the golf scores got out.

Whereas the other secret project was all about image processing.

Our task was to port Logica's LUCID image processing product onto a GEMSTONE console and use an Analogic digital array processor to accelerate the processing functions. I also got to purchase both bits of kit so some nice lunches with salesmen were involved. So, basically we had to take some existing software and make it use some high tech kit including what I can only describe as a Star Trek console and play with aerial/satellite imagery. I was 27 and had so many blinking lights, buttons and yellow trackballs to play with and a dedicated VAX of my own. Did I mention this was the highpoint of my tech career? Plus, the system was delivered to and acceptance tested at a very cool defence establishment. So, as well as the tech I got trips to Portland for the Sonar and Cambridgeshire for the image processing, both in a company hired Fiesta XR2. Vroom vroom!

These projects having been successful I was ready, finally, to go Germany to work on Space stuff. My boss said yes provided I'd do one more important thing for him first. We had 3 months to design and bid for a new system for HMG (as the secret squirrels were referred to in those days). It was worth a lot of money and had some novel aspects and I had no choice anyway. So, London commuting for me for the next 3 months to another secret office. An experienced PM was assigned (who, er, worked through his honeymoon!), I was in charge of the software solution and we had 4 others on the team. I was put on a Yourdon training course, my first experience of a design method, and told to come up with the logical and physical models for the system, working with the hardware guru (who became a friend). Honestly, hadn't a scoobies what I was doing, we presented to the customer, the work was won and I got to go to Germany!

Where my initial assignment was as part of the maintenance team for the Hipparcos satellite control system. This was a Fortran system running on another VAX so nice familiar tech but allowed me to learn how a satellite mission control system worked.

More interesting was the fact that we had two dumb terminals on our desks. One was of course for the VAX to tweak and fix the software. The other was a portal to VM/Profs as I believe it was called. And this, in 1990, was my first experience of Email and social networking (sort of). The implementation was across the European Space Agency's sites and we could look people up in a directory before either calling or emailing them. Cool! Also, we could book videos (VHS cassettes) for the evening from the video club amongst other things. I believe VM/Profs runs on an IBM mainframe which presumably ESA used for its admin and finance.

I was then asked to oversee a team from Science Systems who were developing an update to the Spacecraft Operating System kernel known as SCOS. This allowed Spacecraft Controllers (Spacons) to monitor the satellite's parameters and send commands through a fixed series of fields on a screen and had been in use for several years.

The Science Systems' team were, radically, introducing the concept of WIMPS - windows, icons and mouse pointers on Solaris workstations which ran a version of Unix. This was unheard of tech and my job was to test it worked and introduce it to the control rooms where Spacons could complain about it being different and therefore horrible. I'm pretty sure they've remained WIMPy ever since.

My last job at the European Space Operations Centre was to set the course for the majority of the rest of my career. I was project manager of the 12 person international team put together to build the new spacecraft control system for ISO (the Infrared Space Observatory). The design method used was not Yourdon as I'd hoped but the one ESOC had been using for years, the development remained in Fortran on a VAX and I mostly did management (I did design and develop one subsystem). I have done bits of design and code since but mostly my roles from here on have been increasingly management of others who actually did the tech work.

Whilst living in Germany I wrote a version of Tetris on my Commodore Plus4 in machine code which I was quite proud of. Keith helped me test it during a visit. It worked!

Upon returning to the UK, I joined a very large project by the name of ALFENS which was to provide a low flying booking system for the RAF. I led the small team working out how to glue the system together using a DEC transaction management system ACMS. The system was an early implementation of a distributed system in which the users (pilots) would use Unix workstations to draw their intended routes on maps (all very new) and send the requests as transactions onto a central database. In fact, the approach was so new that it failed and a huge team of 50 was closed down and a core team of 12 retained to come up with a new more workable design. Whilst this was happening, I implemented an emulator in Ada and rebuilt the ACMS tool to manage the simpler transactions resulting from beefing up the workstations.

Two of us then took the lessons learned onto another DEC based transaction management system aimed (laudably) at the idea of collating plans for roadworks in the UK by implementing a Streetworks Register. This time I was team leader of the "back end" processing, capturing the requirements, writing the functional specification and creating the Oracle Database and another ACMS system to handle the requests. This project was dogged by politics and ended up with DEC going to court!

My main lesson from this period was that large fixed price projects suck and the sector hadn't really worked out how to do them yet, especially not with "breakthrough" technologies.

Although not as "hands-on" from a programming perspective, I did get to enjoy further iterations of Tech capability, both at home and at work although many of these are, of course, increasingly common to what has become "normal life"

In Malaysia (1996) I received my first mobile phone (a motorola). These were provided by work to the whole team as the best way for us to keep in touch with each other and the office. I also had a Fax machine at home to send confidential reports! I think this is when I received my first (red screened) laptop too although I did see such things when I was in Germany. Indeed, a colleague was working on one with a touch screen and (terrible) handwriting recognition. By which I mean the recognition was terrible, not that it could recognise terrible handwriting as I was clearly able to demonstrate.

At Science Systems I managed (and tested) a complex project using the ILOG scheduler/solver and views products, again running on UNIX servers and workstations. I also got involved in managing the production of Science Systems' largest (at the time, possibly ever?) project which undertook the heretical exercise of developing and delivering a Spacecraft Control System on Microsoft (PCs and Servers). Common enough now but very risky in 1998. This also used Gensym G2 for automation which got me trips to Barcelona and Boston (Mass).

Future projects involved middle layers, object brokers, auto code generation, Java, swing, beans and various other internetty things but as you can tell, I didn't get too close to the workings of these. My role was often to point out that, clever as the code or application or tool might be, the end result wasn't what the user actually needed or asked for (these things often being different!) so please try again.

But to end on the tech/toys front where I started this chapter, in 2000 I was given (OK asked for) a Tungsten T2 as my first PDA which I loved and still have (but can't charge up). This had a diary, contacts and the ability to take (quite sophisticated) notes either using the hieroglyphic pen entry or a detachable keyboard.

This was my travel companion of choice before mini iPads appeared on the scene. Both being so much lighter and pocket friendly than a bulky laptop.

After the T2 I went through a series of increasingly sophisticated smart phones (most from HTC) which over the years added email, GPS positioning, maps, music and a camera to the basic phone functionality (as I had been hoping they would!).

This then takes us into the realm of iPhones from the 3 to the XR. I currently use an iPhone 8 Red because it's the right size and, er, red! And of course, iPads. I had a very early iPad as part of the @SPARK Room in 2011 and became a convert and advocate of these as "the future".

Home Tech? Not so cutting edge I'm afraid. I have a PS3 because it was brilliant, especially the ability to upgrade its capability through software (DVD->Blu-Ray->3-D!) and it remains our DVD player. Couldn't see the point of the PS4 (not being a "gamer").

For games we all enjoy the Nintendo Switch which is another lovely, easy to use bit of kit. We have a Nest for internet control of heating but have yet to embrace the whole "control your home from your device ethos, though I'm sure that's coming" and Alexa and Siri play their part in our home.

iPodery and streaming music have been part of our lives since around 2007 and currently deciding whether I need both Spotify, Apple and Amazon for this! (Clearly the answer is "no"!)

And to round off with a final example of me lacking Dad's tech vision.... we also have streaming of video over the internet onto our large flat screen Ultra High Def Telly. Well done Dad! I don't know whether he would have seen the potential for video streaming over the internet but, frankly I didn't think that would be possible. But there again, and don't let on, I don't really know how the Internet is possible. Magic?

What's that? Do I still programme? Well, yes in that it has returned to being the hobby it was when I first got hooked. I dabbled in BASIC on my mini-iPad but more recently I have acquired a shiny MacBook which hosts the Xcode App Development Environment and I am plodding my way through PYTHON and the SWIFT programming languages. Watch out for those killer Apps in future!

And that's it for Tech, unless you count watches and cars....

The Now Years

Since leaving the Catapult I have become relaxed! Won't say I sleep much better (guess that's more about aging) but have certainly shaken the anxiety in the pit of the stomach!

Plus, I get to spend more time with my lovely ladies which is fab. For the avoidance of doubt my lovely ladies include Mum, Karen, Kathryn, Jennifer and Becky (in the order I met them).

So, what am I doing with myself? Well, a fair amount of "nothing", sitting enjoying not going to EMT (the Catapult weekly Management Meetings), not panicking when my phone buzzes, drinking tea and coffee in my swivel chair, reading and playing games on my phone. Also:

Creativity

I have a bonkers brain. It throws up ideas and nonsense all the time. Especially at night! But also, when walking alone, at which time I can get it to settle on one topic for a while. Which fuels my creative side!

I enjoyed programming as a kid and I have returned to it with a MacBook. I have just about managed to write an IOS App using Swift but didn't really enjoy it (all form filling and faffery) so have returned to BASIC (via a bit of Python – might have to try that again). In BASIC, I have written a multiplayer version of Yahtzee and an adventure/dungeon game. Nothing to set the world alight but my kind of programming and I really enjoyed writing them. Becky and Kathryn also seem to like playing them so must be OK!

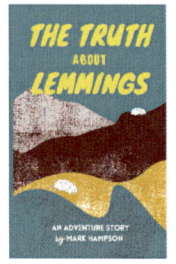

I have written (and self-published on Amazon) my first book. This took around 3 months of hill walkng (!) and is entitled The Truth About Lemmings (aka The Lay of the Lemmings). I am very proud of this as it "reads like a proper book", has "interesting and developed characters" and makes people laugh and cry (in the right places). Onwards and upwards.

I have also written this semi-autobiography of course which has taken best part of 2 years on and off! And a series of lectures on the Physics that I find interesting and would like to share with people.

Walking

Love walking, especially up hills! Have found several new trails over, and aspects of, Bromham Hill which rises a mighty 400 feet above us. Absolutely love it and have now walked it in all seasons. The "Rills" (my name for the crinkly bits) are stunning in sunshine and the meadows on top glorious in Spring. The woodland offers a different ambience and frost and snow in Winter are of course glorious. Rain induced mud is the only killer! That and the Hawks which refuse to be photographed!

There are many other walks available from the doorstep including the 3 Estates around the village of Lacock (Spye Park, Bowden and Bowood) which provide an epic 12 miler including 4 pubs. Can't be bad!

In addition, there are trips to the coast and to the Brecon Beacons to provide more challenging hikes. Plus, of course, we have our cottage in Exmoor where again there are stunning walks from the door in Timberscombe. Up over Dunkery Beacon and down the other side into Horner's woods being up there with the 12 mile best of them!

But for sheer "wowness" it has to be the 4 straight weeks in the Lake District in April/May 2021. Just blissful and amongst many, many walks, the standouts have to be Scafell Pike, Helvellyn via Striding Edge, (plus Blencathra via Sharp Edge on a previous visit!), Skiddaw the interesting way, Great Gable and the Fairfield Round. The latter makes the cut partly for its magnificent views of Striding Edge but mostly cos I did it in Snow on a sunny day! Just beguiling. Did many of the walks with Becky and/or Jennifer which was lovely. Here I am on Striding Edge up to Helvellyn, note the snow sheep!

Travels

Which, thus far, have been seriously hampered by COVID! Shortly after packing up work I ordered a Japanese Import Mitsubishi DELICA SPACE GEAR 3.0 V6 Chamonix (called Mitzi for short) to offer flexible motoring. She can carry 8 people, or turn into a slightly bumpy bed. She can go seriously off road with her high and low ratio fixed differential 4WD and has room inside for all essential camping gear. Thus far she has done a number of day trips with picnics, many trips to the tip, carried Kathryn's gear around and been camped in on trips to mid wales, Brecon Beacons and Norfolk. More is hopefully to follow. I also bought a lightweight drone and decent Nokia camera to use on adventures which have also had limited use so far (although that includes some fab moon photos and look down pictures of Bromham).

Trips to the Alps, New Zealand, South America etc remain in the planning stage as we await the liberation from COVID. Fingers crossed!

Tennis and Golf

Two years in and barely got started with these! 2022 might offer more!

Gardening

Work in progress!! Though we do now have a path through our lower level and a superb Sunroom (kind of conservatory meets orangerie) which was built for us in 2021.

Moon Photo

Cars

Favourite so far ☺............................………Favourite still to come ☺

People and Places

The following table is a simple list of interesting people I've met and places I've been through my career. Most of these will have had a mention somewhere above, but this was my aide memoire for writing the above and is more complete.

Who/Where	What
Tower bridge, North Tower	Meeting with Pew and others to discuss tackling illegal fishing. There is a (very Victorian) meeting room on the first floor of the North Tower of Tower Bridge. Cool!
Foreign & Commonwealth Office, Whitehall	Meeting with FCO and environmental groups such as Zoological Society of London to discuss monitoring of oceans, especially British Indian Ocean territories. The room was a splendid "classic" example with painted ceilings, chandeliers and so on in the heart of Whitehall
British Museum	Behind the scenes meeting in the working areas of the museum to discuss the possibility of detecting ISIS demolition or removal of antiquities from space. Benches, maps, exhibits everywhere, people working with brushes, magnifying glasses etc plus huge library spaces.
The City	At SciSys had many trips to the City of London for investor meetings, including at Canary Wharf and Tower 42 plus many others
Institute of Directors	Many meetings, occasional lunches and drinks at the IoD on Pall Mall (and nice walking around there, admiralty buildings, Trafalgar Square and so on)
UK Space annual Christmas "do"s	Super posh stately rooms in Lancaster house, chatting with the great and the good of the space industry, space agency and usually minister for science over drinks and nibbles.
Beagle 2 Press Event	In very stately rooms in Marlborough House, with Prof Pillinger and Alex James of Blur. Chatted with both.
Department for International Trade	Meeting of its worldwide network for Science and Innovation (SIN) group at the Royal Society in Carlton House
JARIC, GCHQ, MI5	Visited these on several occasions for meetings and did work for 2 of them
World Bank and Inter-American Development Bank in DC	Visited twice, to explain what is possible with satellites (and innovation) and to position UK/Catapults for procurement. Both huge buildings with enormous Atriums.
Spanish embassy DC	Evening reception after World Bank day. Strange combination of modern cellar and olde world pub in quiet street off Pennsylvania Avenue
Evening receptions at the Ambassadors residences	Several times at the residence in Santiago, Chile hosted by Ambassador Fiona Clouder (despite being in her "bad books"), and once in Mexico City and Bogota, Colombia as part of a trade visit
Embassies in Chile & Malaysia	Ran a couple of meetings in the Embassy in Chile and visited the British High Commission in KL on a number of occasions
Chile embassy in London	In Old Queen Street, just off birdcage walk to meet the ambassador to discuss export opportunities around innovation.
National Space Centre in Leicester	Attended launch of Beagle 2 at the Ops room which was hosted at the NSC. Also worked with NSC creative team including Space STEM outreach expert Anu Oja to deliver education workshop (part of my Space 4 Everyone programme) and to commission them to crate the ISIC opening video.
National Physical Laboratory, Teddington	Visited to discuss their involvement in ISIC (provision of Dark Fibre with timing information). Had tour including the Atomic Clocks.
Universities	Visited and worked with various departments in Oxford, Surrey, Reading, Warwick, Imperial College as well as Met Office in Exeter
Lloyd's of London, Boston Room	Met there to discuss satellites with the Chair and his team prior to his visiting Harwell (with his wife). Fab "old fashioned" room built on the 11th floor under the Atrium of the super modern lloyd's building.
Overseas ministers	Communications in Mexico, Agriculture and Fisheries in Colombia and Chile, Transport, Mining, Foreign Affairs, Defence and Finance in Chile including at the National Congress Building
Houston Medical Center	As part of discussions on Satellite Applications at Rice University, was taken to Houston Medical Centre to discuss "Pumps and Pipes". Astonishing place, seemed to comprise 4 hospitals, teaching and research facilities and looked like a city of tower blocks in its own right. Robotic surgery & companion bot.
Houston	Hosted a Life Sciences Spark workshop in Rice University for applications, included David Alexander OBE and NASA AMES people. Dinner with the High Commissioner that evening. Several visits to High Commission Office to discuss opportunities with the DIT team and Houston Chamber of Business (plus discussions around Houston Spaceport)
Denver and Florida	Hosted a group of 6 MPs (including Alan Griffith and Mark Garnier) to visit Space facilities in Denver (Spaceport and Reaction Engines) and in Cape Canaveral (Oneweb, launch pads, Space X, Blue Horizons et al– saw launchpad for early Mercury and Apollo missions, inside VAB etc)

Boston, Harvard and Barcelona	Visited for Gensym Conferences, hosted in Harvard one year and Barcelona another. Looked around Boston with Jeanne (chowder incident) and walked Las Ramblas in Barcelona.
Las Vegas	Visited for Hexagon Conference, in the Venice hotel, amazing size and glitz including indoor canals and St Mark's square! Walked the strip and enjoyed night out in Fremont Street with illuminated roof and zip wires.
World Humanitarian Summit, Istanbul	Huge 3 days event, mostly meeting with Lockheed Martin and others to discuss space enabled disaster response app. I left one discussion with Sean Penn the actor (seemed a genuine guy). Recip Erdogan closed the event. Scary man! Looked around Istanbul, fabulous! Got lost and shared taxi with Mafia man, less so. Nightmare airport/taxi trip in (4am arrival) and airport bombed a week later.
Visited for meetings whilst at Catapult not mentioned elsewhere	EC in Brussels. Glasgow, Cardiff, Edinburgh, Belfast on road shows. Liverpool for conference.
Visited for meetings whilst at SciSys not mentioned elsewhere	Madrid (GMV), Paris (Eutelsat, Thomson, ESA HQ), Rome (Datamat) and Frascati (ESRIN), Noordvijk (ESTEC), Darmstadt (ESOC plus 2 years working and living there), Friedrichshafen (Airbus), Luxemburg (Astra and cricket!)
Chengdu, China	1 week visit with many meetings and visits including new innovation campus, formal meeting with party, board of large high tech company (including dinner). Evening out in old centre and visit to museum.
Kuala Lumpur, Malaysia	Many visits from Catapult as well as lived there for 18 months. Posh hotels, twin towers, KLIA airport (project to help build this!), street markets, lived in Bangsar.
Malaysian Live News programme, AstroAwani.	Live 30 minutes interview to present the EASOS programme. EASOS project was later presented to the PM of Malaysia, Dr Mahathir by our local representatives.
UN Humanitarian Aid discussion	Hosted by me at the Future Cities Catapult in London. Fab venue with meeting rooms in cellars. Took the visitors to a "pub" for traditional dinner; ruined some poor bloke's marriage proposal.
Network Rail Engineering Train, Paddington	Spent 2 hours having a meeting on, and exploring, the bright yellow engineering train which runs about measuring and monitoring the tracks. Proper meeting room in one car, sensors and computers in another.
Operations room at INMARSAT HQ in London.	Many meetings at INMARSAT during the Catapult proposal (nice meeting rooms and cafeteria!) One visit to the Ops room to understand their satellite operations.
House of Commons, Westminster	Several visits for general space meting eg Parliamentary Space Committee with a group of MPs and Space Industry people. Also specific meetings such as the UK Trade Envoys briefing on Catapults, led by me. 12 MPs in meeting room, 6 Catapults presenting.
European Space Agency	Visits to and meetings at ESTEC, the technology Centre in Noordvijk, Netherlands. Also ESRIN, the information centre in Frascati, Italy. Also HQ in Paris. Lived and worked at ESOC (spacecraft Operations) in Darmstadt for 2 years
Government Research Centres	Worked for and meetings at Chemical Defence Establishment (CDE) Porton Down. Worked for and lived at Admiralty Research Establishment (ARE) Portland for 3years.
International Council on Mining Metals, London	Met with chair of ICMM and seniors from several global mining companies to discuss how Satellites could help, especially with environmental impact and disaster prevention.
Williams F1 Technology Centre, Oxfordshire	Took boss of Anglo American mining to an Innovation Event at Williams. Evening reception was in their awesome Formula 1 museum
Nick Clegg, Deputy Prime Minister	Led a trade mission to Colombia and Mexico which I was on. He presented in Spanish which was impressive. Spoke with us at the two garden party/receptions in the Ambassadors' residences.
Vice President of Bolivia	Met and presented to him in Harwell.
Prince Andrew	He opened the ISIC facility at Harwell, Met and had discussion with him in the Spark room about the role of Satellites in the UK's economy.
Malaysian dignitaries	Minister for Transport hosted Airport projects meetings including one overnight meeting where I was negotiating/presenting our budget! Also received invites to "midnight meetings" with him which I turned down! Ex chief of armed forces and Tan Sri responsible for EASOS, controlled armed forces pension fund which owned the fabulous hotel we stayed at. Head of Malaysian Space Agency, Defence University and senior civil servants form Marine, Agriculture, Forestry and mapping departments. Some scary meetings! Presented to 200 people at Malaysian Space Conference (UKSA was a no show, I was on a VIP panel!) and at Defence University. Defence Minister at Farnborough (sat him in a Typhoon cockpit – very pleased).
Head Mexican space agency	Both in Mexico and in Harwell. Discussed cooperation.
Astronaut 1	Met Tim Peake several times at Harwell and at Space events. Spoke at Civil Service Awareness (of space) event in London
Astronaut 2	Met Bob Cabana at Cape Canaveral in his office, currently director of JFK Space Flight Centre! Previous missions include pilot of 2 Space Shuttle Flights and Commander on another 2 including the first deployment to the ISS. Cool talk (with 6 MPs).
Astronaut 3	Met Gene Cernan, Apollo 17 Astronaut and was the last person to walk on the moon. Met him at Rice University in Houston after a workshop we had hosted on UK/US collaboration of Space Life Sciences.

Chilean Presidential visit	Part of a state visit, I was at the evening reception at the Old War Office in Whitehall. Didn't meet (!) but fairly small room of ~100 and she passed within arms length. She was really tiny! We also presented at a "UK innovation showcase" at Imperial College ad I think this was the VP and minister for mines amongst others. Did speak to them!
Crown Prince (now Emperor) Naruhito	He was at Merton (studying Inland Mediaeval waterways!) when I was. Met him with his CID minder outside Merton Bar. I invited him in for a drink and to play darts.
Government Chief scientific advisors	Sir Mark Walport (at Harwell but also in Santiago) and Sir John Beddington.
Senior civil servants (cohorts)	Catapult host several "cohorts" of Senior Civil Servants who were on a week long training course in Oxford for High Flyers. They included people like the MoD Civil Servant responsible for procuring HMS Queen Elizabeth and for rolling out Universal Credit! We presented space capability and innovation to them and then had dinner with them. It was very well received.
Head of met police, sir Bernard Hogan-Howe	Met in the Spark room for a 1 hour meeting that became a 3 hour discussion about the capabilities of Satellites to assist with security and policing. Was followed up with several projects.
At Harwell (ISIC and Catapult) we hosted many VIP and group visits	Groups from France, Peru, Mexico, India, China, Singapore, Oz, NZ, Indonesia, Thailand
Gerry Anderson	Visited the Spark room for a relaxed discussion about Space and Futurology. Signed his name on my iPad!
UK Space Agency	Many visits to 1 Victoria Street (BIS meeting rooms) & Swindon along with Innovate UK at Polaris House.
Posh Dinners on Park Lane	Speakers included William Hague & Bill Bryson
Royal Society for Aerospace Engineers, Park Lane	Number of meetings and presentations, including by me
HMS Dragon, Type 45 destroyer in Valparaiso	Evening reception on board HMS Duncan in Valparaiso Navy Base. Tied up alongside various Chilean (mostly Ex RN) warships. Cocktails, speeches by the Ambassador and the Captain, tour of the ship, Pacific Ocean. Wow.
Logica Paris 20th anniversary celebration	Logica took all its staff (~1,000) to Paris to celebrate its upcoming 20th Anniversary and before it was listed on the stock exchange. It was a drunken and debauched 2 nights and 2 days with River Cruises, Museum visits, posh hotel, two dinners and MANY drinks. Some missed the plane back!
Milton Keynes council	Presented capabilities of Satellites and discussed (28) possible project applications in the council chamber of MK. Led to substantial work, initially on tracking Planning Applications
MPs, Ministers and Lords	A number of MPs at various times, both in House of Commons, at Harwell and other discussions. UK ministers including David Willetts (minister for Science) and Peter Mandelson
Scotland Yard	Several meetings there and at Harwell
Edinburgh	Space medicine with Scottish enterprise, held at innovation hub near university hospital, 50+ attendees. David and I hosted.
Harwell	Met with WWF and BBC to discuss remote monitoring of endangered sites by satellite and by standalone "PODs" part of a WWF campaign which went on to be known as WWF Life. BBC wanted to cover this and were interested in imagery for a series on UK from space, especially seasonal change. We had a particularly fine image showing the whole of the UK under snow – quite rare!
Royal Household	Security detail for royal visits interested in anonymous reconnaissance before visits.
Harwell	Other topics looked at : Nuclear site and transport security (and cooling inlets blocked by jelly fish); city planning, development, environment and pollution; remote healthcare (stroke detection and connected ambulance); technology for security services and police including murder and abduction sites; Hackathons on various topics, globally connected to NASA and ESA sites; Space weather with RAL and Met Office; maritime monitoring with NMIC and MMO; Rail with Network rail & EIT holding board meetings and Spark workshops at Harwell; Road with TRL and DfT; Energy with EDF and big 4 consultancies; Partnership opportunities with Space Florida; Oil and gas with BP and SSTL re RADARSAT constellation; Heathrow airport re on site logistics and snow.

Made in the USA
Columbia, SC
02 April 2023

69986a60-4ff7-4d73-bd7b-baa2de8bf75dR04